Art Power

Art Power

Boris Groys

The MIT Press   Cambridge, Massachusetts   London, England

First MIT Press paperback edition, 2013

© 2008 Boris Groys

This book was set in Garamond and Rotis sans by SNP Best-set Typesetter Ltd., Hong Kong.

Library of Congress Cataloging-in-Publication Data

Groïs, Boris.
Art power / Boris Groys.
   p.   cm.
Includes bibliographical references.
ISBN 978-0-262-07292-2 (hardcover : alk. paper)
ISBN 978-0-262-51868-0 (paperback)
1. Art—Political aspects. 2. Art and state. 3. Art, Modern—20th century—Philosophy.
I. Title.

N72.P6G76   2008
701′.03—dc22   2007020844

Contents

Introduction

The first thing one learns by reading the majority of texts on modern and contemporary art is this: both modern and—even to a greater extent—contemporary art are radically pluralistic. This fact seems to preclude once and for all the possibility of writing on modern art as a specific phenomenon, as a result of the collective work of several generations of artists, curators, and theoreticians—for example, in the same manner in which one would write on Renaissance or Baroque art. At the same time it also precludes the description of any particular modern artwork (and here by modern art I also mean contemporary art) as exemplary of the whole of modern art. Every such attempt can be immediately confronted with a counterexample. So the art theoretician seems to be condemned from the beginning to narrow his or her field of interest and to concentrate on specific art movements, schools, and trends, or, even better, on the work of individual artists. The assertion that modern art escapes any generalization is the only generalization that is still allowed. There are nothing but differences as far as the eye can see. So one must make a choice, take sides, be committed—and accept the inevitability of being accused of one-sidedness, of merely advertising for one's favorite artists at the expense of others with the goal of advancing their commercial success on the art market. In other words: The alleged pluralism of modern and contemporary art makes any discourse on it ultimately futile and frustrating. This fact alone is reason enough to put the dogma of pluralism in question.

Of course, it is true that every modern art movement has provoked a countermovement, every attempt to formulate a theoretical definition of art has provoked an attempt by the artists to produce an artwork that would escape this definition, and so on. When some artists and art critics found the true source of art in the subjective self-expression of an individual artist, other artists and art critics required that art thematize the objective, material conditions of its production and distribution. When some artists insisted on the autonomy of art, others practiced political engagement. And on a more trivial level: When some artists started to make abstract art, other artists began to be ultra-realistic. So one can say that every modern artwork was conceived with the goal of contradicting all other modern artworks in one way or another. But this, of course, does not mean that modern art thereby became pluralistic, for those artworks that did not contradict others were not recognized as relevant or truly modern. Modern art operated not only as a machine of inclusion of everything that was not regarded as art before its emergence but also as a machine of exclusion of everything that imitated already existing art patterns in a naive, unreflective, unsophisticated—nonpolemical—manner, and also of everything that was not somehow controversial, provocative, challenging. But this means: *The field of modern art is not a pluralistic field but a field strictly structured according to the logic of contradiction.* It is a field where every thesis is supposed to be confronted with its antithesis. In the ideal case the representation of thesis and antithesis should be perfectly balanced so that they sum to zero. Modern art is a product of the Enlightenment, and of enlightened atheism and humanism. The death of God means that there is no power in the world that could be perceived as being infinitely more powerful than any other. Thus the atheistic, humanistic, enlightened, modern world believes in the balance of power—and modern art is an expression of this belief. The belief in the balance of power has a regulatory character—and hence modern art has its own power, its own stance: It favors anything that establishes or maintains the balance of power and tends to exclude or try to outweigh anything that distorts this balance.

In fact, art always attempted to represent the greatest possible power, the power that ruled the world in its totality—be it divine or natural power. Thus, as its representation, art traditionally drew its own authority from this power. In this sense art has always been directly or indirectly critical because it confronts finite, political power with images of the infinite—God, nature, fate, life, death. Now the modern state also proclaims the balance of power to be its ultimate goal—but, of course, never truly achieves it. So one can say that modern art in its totality tries to offer an image of the utopian balance of power that exceeds the imperfect balancing power of the state. Hegel, who was the first to celebrate the force of the balance of power embodied by the modern state, believed that in modernity art had become a thing of the past. That is, he couldn't imagine that the balance of power could be shown, could be presented as an image. He believed that the true balance of power, having zero as its sum, could only be thought, not seen. But modern art has shown that is also possible to visualize the zero, the perfect balance of power.

If there is no image that could function as a representation of an infinite power, then all images are equal. And, indeed, contemporary art has the equality of all the images as its *telos*. But the equality of all images exceeds the pluralistic, democratic equality of aesthetic taste. There is always an infinite surplus of possible images that do not correspond to any specific taste, be it an individual taste, "high" taste, marginal taste, or the taste of the masses. Therefore, it is also always possible to refer to this surplus of unwanted, unliked images—and that is what contemporary art continually does. Already Malevich said that he was struggling against the sincerity of the artist. And Broodthaers said—when he started to do art—that he wanted to do something insincere. To be insincere means in this context to make art beyond all taste—even beyond one's own taste. Contemporary art is an excess of taste, including the pluralistic taste. In this sense it is an excess of pluralistic democracy, an excess of democratic equality. This excess both stabilizes and destabilizes the democratic balance of taste and power at the same time. This paradox is, actually, what characterizes contemporary art in its totality.

And it is not only the field of art in its totality that can be seen as an embodiment of paradox. Already in the framework of classical modernity, but especially in the context of contemporary art, individual artworks began to be paradox-objects that embody simultaneously thesis and antithesis. Thus *Fountain* by Duchamp is artwork and non-artwork at the same time. Also, *Black Square* by Malevich is both a mere geometrical figure and a painting at the same time. But the artistic embodiment of self-contradiction, of paradox, began to be especially practiced in contemporary art after World War II. At this point we are confronted with paintings that could be described as both realistic and abstract at the same time (Gerhard Richter), or objects that can be described as both traditional sculptures and as readymades at the same time (Fischli/Weiss), to mention just a few examples. We are also confronted with artworks that aim to be both documentary and fictional, and with artistic interventions that want to be political, in the sense of transcending the borders of the art system—while at the same time remaining within these borders. The number of such contradictions and of contemporary artworks that represent and actually embody these contradictions seems as if it can be increased at will. These artworks may create the illusion that they invite the spectator to a potentially infinite plurality of interpretations, that they are open in their meaning, that they do not impose on the spectator any specific ideology, or theory, or faith.

But this appearance of infinite plurality is, of course, only an illusion. De facto there is only one correct interpretation that they impose on the spectator: as paradox-objects, these artworks require a perfectly paradoxical, self-contradictory reaction. Any nonparadoxical or only partially paradoxical reaction should be regarded in this case as reductive and, in fact, false. The only adequate interpretation of a paradox is a paradoxical interpretation. Thus the deeper difficulty in dealing with modern art consists in our unwillingness to accept paradoxical, self-contradictory interpretations as adequate and true. But this unwillingness should be overcome—so that we can see modern and contemporary art for what it is, namely, a site of revelation of the paradox governing the balance of power. In fact, to be a paradox-object is the normative requirement implicitly applied to any contemporary artwork. A contemporary artwork is as good as it is paradoxical—as it is capable of embodying the most radical self-contradiction, as it is capable of contributing to establishing and maintaining the perfect balance of power between thesis and antithesis. In this sense even the most radically one-sided artworks can be regarded as good if they help to redress the distorted balance of power in the field of art as a whole.

Being one-sided and aggressive is, of course, at least as modern as being moderate and seeking to maintain the balance of power. The modern revolutionary, or, one might say, totalitarian movements and states are also aiming at the balance of power, but they believe that it can be found only in and through permanent struggle, conflict and war. The art that is put in the service of such a dynamic, revolutionary balance of power takes necessarily the form of political propaganda. Such art does not reduce itself to the representation of power—it participates in the struggle for power that it interprets as the only way in which the true balance of power could reveal itself. Now I must confess that my own essays collected in this book are also motivated by a wish to contribute to a certain balance of power in today's art world—namely, to find more space in it for art functioning as political propaganda.

Under the conditions of modernity an artwork can be produced and brought to the public in two ways: as a commodity or as a tool of political propaganda. The amounts of art produced under these two regimes can be seen as roughly equal. But under the conditions of the contemporary art scene, much more attention is devoted to the history of art as commodity and much less to art as political propaganda. The official as well as unofficial art of the Soviet Union and of other former Socialist states remains almost completely out of focus for the contemporary art history and museum system. The same can be said of the state-supported art of Nazi Germany or Fascist Italy. The same can also be said of Western European art that was supported and propagated by the Western Communist parties, especially by the French Communist Party. The only exception is the art of Russian Constructivism that was created under NEP, during the temporary reintroduction of the limited free market in Soviet Russia. Of course, there is a reason for this neglect of the politically motivated art that was produced outside the standard conditions of the art market: After the end of World War II and especially after the change of regime in the former Socialist Eastern European countries, the commercial system of art production and distribution dominated the political system. The notion of art became almost synonymous with the notion of the art market, so that the art produced under the nonmarket conditions was de facto excluded from the field of institutionally recognized art. This ongoing exclusion is usually expressed in moral terms: One seems to be too ethically concerned to deal with the "totalitarian" art of the twentieth century that "perverted" the "genuine" political aspirations of true utopian art. This notion of "perverted art" as distinct from "genuine art" is, of course, highly problematic—in a very curious way this vocabulary is used time and again by authors who are quick to denounce the use of the same notion of perversion in other contexts. It is also interesting that even the most severe judgment on the moral dimensions of the free market never leads anybody to conclude that art that was and is produced under those market conditions should be excluded from critical and historical consideration. It is also characteristic of this mindset that not only the official but also the unofficial, dissident art of the Socialist countries tends to be neglected by the dominating art theory.

But whatever one may think about the moral dimension of nonmarket, "totalitarian" art is, in fact, of no relevance here. The representation of this politically motivated art inside the art world has nothing to do with the question of whether one finds this art morally or even aesthetically good or bad—just as nobody would ask whether Duchamp's *Fountain* is morally or aesthetically good or bad. As readymade, the commodity gained unlimited access to the art world—but political propaganda did not. In this way the balance of power between economy and politics in art has become distorted. One cannot, that is, avoid the suspicion that the exclusion of art that was not produced under the standard art market conditions has only one ground: The dominating art discourse identifies art with the art market and remains blind to any art that is produced and distributed by any mechanism other than the market.

Significantly, this understanding of art is also shared by the majority of those artists and art theoreticians who aim to be critical of the commodification of art—and who want art itself to be critical of its own commodification. But to perceive the critique of commodification as the main or even unique goal of contemporary art is just to reaffirm the total power of the art market—even if this reaffirmation takes a form of critique. Art is understood on this perspective as completely powerless, lacking any immanent criteria of choice and immanent logic of development. According to this type of analysis, the art world is entirely occupied by various commercial interests that "in the last instance" dictate the criteria of inclusion and exclusion that shape the art world. The artwork presents itself in this perspective as an unhappy, suffering commodity, one that is utterly submissive to the power of the market and differentiates itself from other commodities only through its ability to become a critical and self-critical commodity. And this notion of a self-critical commodity is, of course, utterly paradoxical. The (self-)critical artwork is a paradox-object that fits perfectly in the dominating paradigm of modern and contemporary art. There is, therefore, nothing to say against this kind of (self-)critical art from within that paradigm—but the question arises if such art can also be understood as truly political art.

Of course, everybody who is involved in any kind of art practice or criticism is interested in these questions: Who decides what is art and what is not art? And who decides what is good art and what is bad art? Is it the artist, the curator, the art critic, the collector, the art system as a whole, the art market, the general public? But it seems to me that this question, though tempting, is nevertheless wrong-headed. Whoever decides anything about art can make mistakes; the general, democratic public can make mistakes—and in fact has made them already many times in its history. We should not forget that all avant-garde art was made against public taste—even and especially when it was made in the name of public taste. That means: The democratization of the art audience is not an answer. And the education of the public is also not an answer, because all good art always was and still is made against any kind of rules put forth by education. A critique of the existing art market rules and art institutions is, of course, legitimate and necessary, but this critique makes sense only if its goal is to draw our attention to interesting or relevant art that is overlooked by these institutions. And, as all of us know well, if this kind of critique is successful it leads to the inclusion of the overlooked art in these institutions—and, therefore, ultimately, to the further stabilization of these institutions. The internal critique of the art market is able to improve it to a degree—but it is not able to change it fundamentally.

Art becomes politically effective only when it is made beyond or outside the art market—in the context of direct political propaganda. Such art was made in the former Socialist countries. Current examples include the Islamist videos or posters that are functioning in the context of the international antiglobalist movement. Of course, this kind of art gets economic support from the state or from various political and religious movements. But its production, evaluation, and distribution do not follow the logic of the market. This kind of art is not a commodity. Especially under the rules of the Socialist economy of the Soviet type, artworks were not commodities, because there was no market at all. These artworks were not created for individual consumers who were supposed to be their potential buyers, but for the masses who should absorb and accept their ideological message.

Of course, one can easily argue that such propaganda art is simply political design- and image-making. And that means that in the context of political propaganda, art remains as powerless as it is in the context of the art market. This judgment is in a sense both true and untrue. Of course, the artists working in the context of propaganda art are not—speaking in the idiom of contemporary management—content providers. They are making advertisements for a certain ideological goal—and they subordinate their art to this goal. But what is, actually, this goal itself? Every ideology is based on a certain "vision," on a certain image of the future—be it an image of paradise, Communist society, or permanent revolution. And this is what signals the fundamental difference between market commodities and political propaganda. The market operates by an "invisible hand," it is merely a dark suspicion; it circulates images, but it does not have its own image. By contrast, the power of an ideology is always ultimately the power of a vision. And this means that by serving any political or religious ideology an artist ultimately serves art. That is why an artist can also challenge a regime based on an ideological vision in a much more effective way than he or she can challenge the art market. An artist operates on the same territory as ideology. The affirmative and critical potential of art demonstrates itself, therefore, much more powerfully and productively in the context of politics than in the context of the market.

At the same time, the artwork remains under the ideological regime a paradox-object. That is, every ideological vision is only a promised image—an image of what is to come. The materialization, realization of the ideological vision must be always postponed—to the apocalyptic end of history, or to the coming community of the future. Thus all ideologically motivated art necessarily breaks with this politics of deferral, because art is always made here and now. Of course, ideologically motivated art can always be interpreted as prefiguration, as anticipation of the true vision to come. But this art can also be seen at the same time as a parody, critique, denigration of this vision—as evidence that nothing will change in the world even if the ideological vision becomes flesh. The substitution of the ideological vision by the artwork is the substitution of the sacred time of infinite hope by the profane time of archives and historical memory. After the faith in the promised vision is lost, it is art that remains. This means that all ideologically motivated art—be it religious, Communist, or Fascist—is always already affirmative and critical at the same time. Every realization of a certain project—be it religious, ideological, or technical—is always also a negation of this project, a termination of this project as project. Every artwork that presents a vision that is guiding a certain religious or political ideology makes this vision profane—and thus becomes a paradox-object.

Now, ideologically motivated art is not simply a thing of the past or of marginal ideological and political movements. Today's mainstream Western art also functions increasingly in the mode of ideological propaganda. This art is also made and exhibited for the masses, for those who do not necessarily wish to purchase it—indeed, the nonbuyers constitute the overwhelming and ever-increasing audience for art as it is regularly shown at the well-known international biennials, triennials, and so on. These exhibitions should not be mistaken for mere sites of self-presentation and glorification of the values of the art market. Rather, they try time and again to both create and demonstrate a balance of power between contradictory art trends, aesthetic attitudes, and strategies of representation—to give an idealized, curated image of this balance.

The struggle against the power of ideology traditionally took the form of struggle against the power of the image. Anti-ideological, critical, enlightened thought has always tried to get rid of images, to destroy or, at least, to deconstruct them—with the goal of replacing images with invisible, purely rational concepts. The announcement made by Hegel that art is a thing of the past and that our epoch has become the epoch of the Concept was a proclamation of victory of the iconoclastic Enlightenment over Christian iconophilia. Of course, Hegel was right at the time to make this diagnosis, but he overlooked the possibility of conceptual art. Modern art has demonstrated time and again its power by appropriating the iconoclastic gestures directed against it and by turning these gestures into new modes of art production. The modern artwork positioned itself as a paradox-object also in this deeper sense—as an image and as a critique of the image at the same time.

This has guaranteed art a chance of survival under the conditions of radical secularization and de-ideologization—in a perspective that goes far beyond that of being a mere commodity on the art market. Our allegedly postideological age also has its own image: the prestigious international exhibition as the image of the perfect balance of power. The desire to get rid of any image can be realized only through a new image—the image of a critique of the image. This fundamental figure—the artistic appropriation of iconoclasm that produces the paradox-objects we call modern works of art—is the subject, either directly or indirectly, of the essays that follow.

Part I

The Logic of Equal Aesthetic Rights

If we want to speak about the ability of art to resist external pressure, the following question must first be answered: Does art have its own territory that is worthy of being defended? The autonomy of art has been denied in many recent art-theoretical discussions. If these discourses are right, art cannot be a source of any resistance whatsoever. In the best case art could be used merely for designing, for aestheticizing the already existent oppositional, emancipatory political movements—that is, it could be at best merely a supplement to politics. This seems to me to be the crucial question: Does art hold any power of its own, or it is only able to decorate external powers—whether these are powers of oppression or liberation? Thus the question of the autonomy of art seems to me the central question in the context of any discussion on the relationship between art and resistance. And my answer to this question is: Yes, we can speak about the autonomy of art; and, yes, art does have an autonomous power of resistance.

Of course, that art has such an autonomy does not mean that the existing art institutions, art system, art world, or art market can be seen as autonomous in any significant sense of the word. For the functioning of the art system is based on certain aesthetic value judgments, on certain criteria of choice, rules of inclusion and exclusion, and the like. All these value judgments, criteria, and rules are, of course, not autonomous. Rather, they reflect the dominant social conventions and power structures. We can safely say: There is no such thing as a purely aesthetic, art-immanent, autonomous value system that could regulate the art world in its entirety. This insight has brought many artists and theorists to the conclusion that art as such is not autonomous, because the autonomy of art was—and still is—thought of as dependent on the autonomy of the aesthetic value judgment. But I would suggest that it is precisely this absence of any immanent, purely aesthetic value judgment that guarantees the autonomy of art. The territory of art is organized around the lack or, rather, the rejection of any aesthetic judgment. Thus the autonomy of art implies not an autonomous hierarchy of taste—but abolishing every such hierarchy and establishing the regime of equal aesthetic rights for all artworks. The art world should be seen as the socially codified manifestation of the fundamental equality between all visual forms, objects, and media. Only under this assumption of the fundamental aesthetic equality of all artworks can every value judgment, every exclusion or inclusion, be potentially recognized as a result of a heteronomous intrusion into the autonomous sphere of art—as the effect of pressure exercised by external forces and powers. And it is this recognition that opens up the possibility of resistance in the name of art's autonomy, that is, in the name of the equality of all art forms and media. But, of course, I mean "art" to be understood as the result of a long battle for recognition that took place over the course of modernity.

Art and politics are initially connected in one fundamental respect: both are realms in which a struggle for recognition is being waged. As defined by Alexander Kojève in his commentary on Hegel, this struggle for recognition surpasses the usual struggle for the distribution of material goods, which in modernity is generally regulated by market forces. What is at stake here is not merely that a certain desire be satisfied but that it also be recognized as socially legitimate.[1] Whereas politics is an arena in which various group interests have, both in the past and the present, fought for recognition, artists of the classical avant-garde have mostly contended for the recognition of individual forms and artistic procedures that were not previously considered legitimate. The classical avant-garde has struggled to achieve recognition of all signs, forms, and things as legitimate objects of artistic desire and, hence, also as legitimate objects of representation in art. Both forms of struggle are intrinsically bound up with each other, and both have as their aim a situation in which all people with their various interests, as indeed also all forms and artistic procedures, will finally be granted equal rights.

Already the classical avant-garde has opened up the infinite horizontal field of all possible pictorial forms, which are all lined up alongside one another with equal rights. One after another, so-called primitive artworks, abstract forms, and simple objects from everyday life have all acquired the kind of recognition that once used to be granted only to the historically privileged artistic masterpieces. This equalizing of art practices has become progressively more pronounced in the course of the twentieth century, as the images of mass culture, entertainment, and kitsch have been accorded equal status within the traditional high art context. At the same time, this politics of equal aesthetic rights, this struggle for aesthetic equality between all visual forms and media that modern art has fought to establish was—and still is even now—frequently criticized as an expression of cynicism and, paradoxically enough, of elitism. This criticism has been directed against modern art both from the right and from the left—as a lack of genuine love for art or as a lack of genuine political involvement, of political engagement. But, in fact, this politics of equal rights on the level of aesthetics, on the level of aesthetic value, is a necessary precondition for any political engagement. Indeed, the contemporary politics of emancipation is a politics of inclusion—directed against the exclusion of political and economical minorities. But this struggle for inclusion is possible only if the forms in which the desires of the excluded minorities manifest themselves are not rejected and suppressed from the beginning by any kind of aesthetical censorship operating in the name of higher aesthetical values. Only under the presupposition of the equality of all visual forms and media on the aesthetic level is it possible to resist the factual inequality between the images—as imposed from the outside, and reflecting cultural, social, political, or economical inequalities.

As Kojève has already pointed out, when the overall logic of equality underlying individual struggles for recognition becomes apparent, it creates the impression that these struggles have to some extent surrendered their true seriousness and explosiveness.[2] This was why even before World War II Kojève was able to speak of the end of history—in the sense of the political history of struggles for recognition. Since then, this discourse about the end of history has made its mark particularly on the art scene. People are constantly referring to the end of art history, by which they mean that these days all forms and things are "in principle" already considered works of art. Under this premise, the struggle for recognition and equality in art has reached its logical end—and therefore become outdated and superfluous. For if, as it is argued, all images are already acknowledged as being of equal value, this would seemingly deprive the artist of the possibility to break taboos, provoke, shock, or extend boundaries of the acceptable. Instead, by the time history has come to an end, each artist begins to be suspected of producing just one further arbitrary image among many. Were this indeed the case, the regime of equal rights for all images would have to be regarded not only as the *telos* of the logic followed by the history of modern art, but also as its terminal negation.

Accordingly, we now witness repeated waves of nostalgia for a time when certain individual works of art were revered as precious, singular masterpieces. On the other hand, many protagonists of the art world believe that now, after the end of art history, the only criterion left for measuring the quality of an individual artwork is its success on the art market. Of course, the artist can also deploy his or her art as a political instrument in the context of various continuing political struggles—as an act of political commitment. But such a political commitment is viewed mostly as being extraneous to art, intent on instrumentalizing art for external political interests and aims. And worse still, such a move may also be dismissed as mere publicity for an artist's work by means of political profile-seeking. This suspicion of commercially exploiting media attention by means of political commitment thwarts even the most ambitious endeavors to politicize art.

But the equality of all visual forms and media in terms of their aesthetic value does not mean an erasure of all differences between good art and bad art. Quite the opposite is the case. Good art is precisely that practice which aims at confirmation of this equality. And such a confirmation is necessary because formal aesthetic equality does not secure the factual equality of forms and media in terms of their production and distribution. One might say that today's art operates in the gap between the formal equality of all art forms and their factual inequality. That is why there can be and is "good art"—even if all artworks have equal aesthetic rights. The good artwork is precisely that work which affirms the formal equality of all images under the conditions of their factual inequality. This gesture is always contextual and historically specific, but it also has paradigmatic importance as a model for further repetitions of this gesture. Thus, social or political criticism in the name of art has an affirmative dimension that transcends its immediate historical context. By criticizing the socially, culturally, politically, or economically imposed hierarchies of values, art affirms aesthetic equality as a guarantee of its true autonomy.

The artist of the *ancien régime* was intent on creating a masterpiece, an image that would exist in its own right as the ultimate visualization of the abstract ideas of truth and beauty. In modernity, on the other hand, artists have tended to present examples of an infinite sequence of images—as Kandinsky did with abstract compositions; as Duchamp did with ready-mades; as Warhol did with icons of mass culture. The source of the impact that these images exerted on subsequent art production lies not in their exclusivity, but instead in their very capacity to function as mere examples of the potentially infinite variety of images. They are not only presenting themselves but also act as pointers to the inexhaustible mass of images, of which they are delegates of equal standing. It is precisely this reference to the infinite multitude of excluded images that lends these individual specimens their fascination and significance within the finite contexts of political and artistic representation.

Hence, it is not to the "vertical" infinity of divine truth that the artist today makes reference, but to the "horizontal" infinity of aesthetically equal images. Without doubt, each reference to this infinity needs to be scrutinized and wielded strategically if its use in any specific representational context is to be effective. Some images that artists insert into the context of the international art scene signal their particular ethnic or cultural origin. These images resist the normative aesthetic control exerted by the current mass media, which shuns all regionality. At the same time, other artists transplant mass-media-produced images into the context of their own regional cultures as a means of escaping the provincial and folkloric dimensions of their immediate milieus. Both artistic strategies initially appear to oppose each other: one approach emphasizes images that denote national cultural identity, while the other, inversely, prefers everything international, globalized, media related. But these two strategies are only ostensibly antagonistic: Both make reference to something that is excluded from a particular cultural context. In the first case, the exclusion discriminates against regional images; the second targets mass media images. But in both instances, the images in question are simply examples that point to the infinite, "utopian" realm of aesthetic equality. These examples could mislead us to conclude that contemporary art always acts *ex negativo*, that its reflex in any situation is to adopt a critical position merely for the sake of being critical. But this is by no means the case: all the examples of a critical position ultimately refer to the single, utterly positive, affirmative, emancipatory, and utopian vision of an infinite realm of images endowed with equal aesthetic rights.

This kind of criticism in the name of aesthetic equality is as necessary now as ever. The contemporary mass media has emerged as by far the largest and most powerful machine for producing images—vastly more extensive and effective than our contemporary art system. We are constantly fed images of war, terror, and catastrophes of all kinds, at a level of production with which the artist with his artisan skills cannot compete. And in the meantime, politics has also shifted to the domain of media-produced imagery. Nowadays, every major politician generates thousands of images through public appearances. Correspondingly, politicians are now also increasingly judged on the aesthetics of their performance. This situation is often lamented as an indication that "content" and "issues" have become masked by "media appearance." But this increasing aestheticization of politics offers us at the same time a chance to analyze and to criticize the political performance in artistic terms. That is, media-driven politics operates on the terrain of art. At first glance the diversity of the media images may appear to be immense, if not nearly immeasurable. If one adds images of politics and war to those of advertising, commercial cinema, and entertainment, it seems that the artist—the last craftsperson of present-day modernity—stands no chance of rivaling the supremacy of these image-generating machines. But in reality, the diversity of images circulating in the media is highly limited. Indeed, in order to be effectively propagated and exploited in the commercial mass media, images need to be easily recognizable for the broad target audience, rendering mass media nearly tautological. The variety of images circulating in the mass media is much more limited than the range of images preserved, for example, in museums or produced by contemporary art. That is why it is necessary to keep the museums and, in general, art institutions as places where the visual vocabulary of the contemporary mass media can be critically compared to the art heritage of the previous epochs and where we can rediscover artistic visions and projects pointing toward the introduction of aesthetic equality.

Museums are increasingly being viewed today with skepticism and mistrust by both art insiders and the general public. On all sides one repeatedly hears that the institutional boundaries of the museum ought to be transgressed, deconstructed, or simply removed to give contemporary art full freedom to assert itself in real life. Such appeals and demands have become quite commonplace, to the extent of now being regarded as a cardinal feature of contemporary art. These calls for the abolition of the museum appear to follow earlier avant-garde strategies and as a result are wholeheartedly embraced by the contemporary art community. But appearances are deceiving. The context, meaning, and function of these calls to abolish the museum system have undergone a fundamental change since the days of the avant-garde, even if at first sight the diction of these calls seems so familiar. Prevailing tastes in the nineteenth and the first part of the twentieth centuries were defined and embodied by the museum. In these circumstances, any protest directed at the museum was simultaneously a protest against the prevailing norms of art-making—and by the same token also the basis from which new, groundbreaking art could evolve. But in our time the museum has indisputably been stripped of its normative role. The general public now draws its notion of art from advertising, MTV videos, video games, and Hollywood blockbusters. In the contemporary context of media-generated taste, the call to abandon and dismantle the museum as an institution has necessarily taken on an entirely different meaning than when it was voiced during the avant-garde era. When people today speak of "real life," what they usually mean is the global media market. And that means: The current protest against the museum is no longer part of a struggle being waged against normative taste in the name of aesthetic equality but is, inversely, aimed at stabilizing and entrenching currently prevailing tastes.

Art institutions, however, are still typically portrayed in the media as places of selection, where specialists, insiders, and the initiated few pass preliminary judgment on what is permitted to rate as art in general, and what in particular is "good" art. This selection process is assumed to be based on criteria that to a wider audience must seem unfathomable, incomprehensible and, in the final estimation, also irrelevant. Accordingly, one wonders why anyone at all is needed to decide what is art and what is not. Why can't we just choose for ourselves what we wish to acknowledge or appreciate as art without looking to an intermediary, without patronizing advice from curators and art critics? Why does art refuse to seek legitimacy on the open market just like any other product? From a mass media perspective, the traditional aspirations of the museum seem historically obsolete, out of touch, insincere, even somewhat bizarre. And contemporary art itself time and again displays an eagerness to follow the enticements of the mass media age, voluntarily abandoning the museum in the quest to be disseminated through media channels. Of course, the readiness on the part of many artists to become involved in the media, in broader public communication and politics—in other words to engage in "real life" beyond the boundaries of the museum—is quite understandable. This kind of opening allows the artists to address and seduce a much larger audience; it is also a decent way of earning money—which the artist previously had to beg for from the state or private sponsors. It gives the artist a new sense of power, social relevance, and public presence rather than forcing him or her to eke out a meager existence as the poor relative of the media. So the call to break loose from the museum amounts de facto to a call to package and commercialize art by accommodating it to the aesthetic norms generated by today's mass media.

The abandonment of the "musealized" past is also often celebrated as a radical opening up to the present. But opening up to the big world outside the closed spaces of the art system produces, on the contrary, a certain blindness to what is contemporary and present. The global media market lacks in particular the historical memory that would enable the spectator to compare the past with the present and thereby determine what is truly new and genuinely contemporary about the present. The product range in the media market is constantly being replaced by new merchandise, barring any possibility of comparing what is on offer today with what used to be available in the past. As a result, the new and the present are discussed in terms of what is in fashion. But what is fashionable is itself by no means self-evident or indisputable. While it is easy to agree that in the age of mass media our lives are dictated predominantly by fashion, how confused we suddenly become when asked to say precisely what is en vogue just now. Who can actually say what is fashionable at any moment? For instance, if something appears to have become fashionable in Berlin, one could quickly point out that this trend has long since gone out of fashion measured against what is currently fashionable in, say, Tokyo or Los Angeles. Yet who can guarantee that the same Berlin fashion won't at some later date also hit the streets of Los Angeles or Tokyo? When it comes to assessing the market, we are de facto at the blind mercy of advice dispensed by market gurus, the purported specialists of international fashion. Yet such advice cannot be verified by any individual consumer since, as everyone knows, the global market is too vast for him or her alone to fathom. Hence, where the media market is concerned one has the simultaneous impression of being bombarded relentlessly with something new and also of permanently witnessing the return of the same. The familiar complaint that there is nothing new in art has the same root as the opposite charge that art is constantly striving to appear new. As long as the media is the only point of reference the observer simply lacks any comparative context which would afford him or her the means of effectively distinguishing between old and new, between what is the same and what is different.

In fact, only the museum gives the observer the opportunity to differentiate between old and new, past and present. For museums are the repositories of historical memory where also images and things are kept and shown that have meanwhile gone out of fashion, that have become old and outdated. In this respect only the museum can serve as the site of systematic historical comparison that enables us to see with our own eyes what really is different, new, and contemporary. The same, incidentally, applies to the assertions of cultural difference or cultural identity that persistently bombard us in the media. In order to challenge these claims critically, we again require some form of comparative framework. Where no such comparison is possible all claims of difference and identity remain unfounded and hollow. Indeed, every important art exhibition in a museum offers such a comparison, even if this is not explicitly enacted, for each museum exhibition inscribes itself into a history of exhibitions that is documented within the art system.

Of course, the strategies of comparison pursued by individual curators and critics can in turn also be criticized, but such a critique is possible only because they too can be measured against the previous curatorial strategies that are kept by the art memory. In other words, the very idea of abandoning or even abolishing the museum would close off the possibility of holding a critical inquiry into the claims of innovation and difference with which we are constantly confronted in today's media. This also explains why the selection criteria manifested by contemporary curatorial projects so frequently differ from those that prevail in the mass media. The issue here is not that curators and art initiates have exclusive and elitist tastes sharply distinct from those of the broad public, but that the museum offers a means of comparing the present with the past that repeatedly arrives at conclusions other than those implied by the media. An individual observer would not necessarily be in a position to undertake such a comparison if the media were all he had to rely on. So it is hardly surprising that the media at the end of the day end up adopting the museum's diagnosis of what exactly is contemporary about the present, simply because they themselves are unable to perform a diagnosis of their own.

Thus today's museums are in fact designed not merely to collect the past, but also to generate the present through the comparison between old and new. The new is here not something merely different but, rather, a reaffirmation of the fundamental aesthetic equality of all the images in a historically given context. The mass media constantly renew the claim to confront the spectator with different, groundbreaking, provocative, true and authentic art. The art system keeps, on the contrary, the promise of aesthetic equality that undermines any such claim. The museum is first and foremost a place where we are reminded of the egalitarian projects of the past and where we can learn to resist the dictatorship of contemporary taste.

On the New

In recent decades, the discourse on the impossibility of the new in art has become especially widespread and influential. Its most interesting character-istic is a certain feeling of happiness, of positive excitement about this alleged end of the new—a certain inner satisfaction that this discourse obviously produces in the contemporary cultural milieu. Indeed, the initial postmodern sorrow about the end of history is gone. Now we seem to be happy about the loss of history, of the idea of progress, of the utopian future—all things traditionally connected to the phenomenon of the new. Liberation from the obligation to be historically new seems to be a great victory of life over for-merly predominant historical narratives which tended to subjugate, ideolo-gize, and formalize reality. Given that we experience art history first of all as represented in our museums, the liberation from the new, understood as liberation from art history—and, for that matter, from history as such—is experienced by the art world in the first place as a chance to break out of the museum. Breaking out of the museum means becoming popular, alive, and present outside the closed circle of the established art world, outside the museum's walls. Therefore, it seems to me that the positive excitement about the end of the new in art is linked in the first place to this promise of bringing art into life—beyond all historical constructions and considerations, beyond the opposition of old and new.

Artists and art theoreticians alike are glad to be free at last from the burden of history, from the necessity to make the next step, and from the obligation to conform to the historical laws and requirements of that which is historically new. Instead, these artists and theoreticians want to be politi-cally and culturally engaged in social reality; they want to reflect on their own cultural identity, express their individual desires, and so on. But first of all they want to show themselves to be truly alive and real—in opposition to the abstract, dead historical constructions represented by the museum system and by the art market. It is, of course, a completely legitimate desire. But to be able to fulfill this desire to make a true living art we have to answer the following question: When and under what conditions does art appear to be most alive?

There is a deep-rooted tradition in modernity of history bashing, museum bashing, library bashing, or more generally, archive bashing in the name of real life. The library and the museum are the preferred objects of intense hatred for a majority of modern writers and artists. Rousseau admired the destruction of the famous ancient Library of Alexandria; Goethe's Faust was prepared to sign a contract with the devil if he could escape the library (and the obligation to read its books). In the texts of modern artists and theoreticians, the museum is repeatedly described as a graveyard of art, and museum curators as gravediggers. According to this tradition, the death of the museum—and of the art history embodied by the museum—must be interpreted as a resurrection of true, living art, as a turning toward true reality, life, toward the great Other: If the museum dies, it is death itself that dies. We suddenly become free, as if we had escaped a kind of Egyptian bondage and were prepared to travel to the Promised Land of true life. All this is quite understandable, even if it is not so obvious *why* the Egyptian captivity of art has come to its end just now.

However, the question I am more interested in at this moment is, as I said, a different one: Why does art want to be alive rather than dead? And what does it mean for art to be alive, or look as if it were alive? I'll try to show that it is the inner logic of museum collecting itself that compels the artist to go into reality—into life—and make art that is seen as being alive. I shall also try to show that "being alive" means, in fact, nothing more or less than being new.

It seems to me that the numerous discourses on historical memory and its representation often overlook the complementary relationship that exists between reality and museum. The museum is not secondary to "real" history, nor is it merely a reflection and documentation of what "really" happened outside its walls according to the autonomous laws of historical development. The contrary is true: "reality" itself is secondary in relation to the museum— the "real" can be defined only in comparison with the museum collection. This means that any change in the museum collection brings about a change in our perception of reality itself—after all, reality can be defined in this context as the sum of all things not yet being collected. So history cannot be understood as a fully autonomous process which takes place outside the museum's walls. Our image of reality is dependent on our knowledge of the museum.

One case clearly shows that the relationship between reality and museum is mutual: the case of the art museum. Modern artists working after the emergence of the modern museum know (in spite of all their protests and resentments) that they are working primarily for the museums' collections—at least if they are working in the context of so-called high art. These artists know from the beginning that they will be collected—and they actually want to be collected. Whereas dinosaurs didn't know that they would eventually be represented in museums of natural history, artists on the other hand know that they may eventually be represented in museums of art history. As much as the behavior of dinosaurs was—at least in a certain sense—unaffected by their future representation in the modern museum, the behavior of the modern artist *is* affected by the knowledge of such a possibility, and in a very substantial way. It is obvious that the museum accepts only things that it takes from real life, from outside of its collections, and this explains why the artist wants to make his or her art look real and alive.

What is already presented in the museum is automatically regarded as belonging to the past, as already dead. If, outside the museum, we encounter something that makes us think of the forms, positions, and approaches already represented inside the museum, we do not see this something as real or alive, but rather as a dead copy of the dead past. So if an artist says (as the majority of artists say) that he or she wants to break out of the museum, to go into life itself, to be real, to make a truly living art, this can only mean that the artist wants to be collected. This is because the only possibility of being collected is by transcending the museum and entering life in the sense of making something different from that which has already been collected. Again: Only the new can be recognized by the museum-trained gaze as real, present, and alive. If you repeat already collected art, your art is qualified by the museum as mere *kitsch* and rejected. Those virtual dinosaurs which are merely dead copies of already museographed dinosaurs could be shown, as we know, in the context of *Jurassic Park*—in the context of amusement, entertainment—but not in the museum. The museum is, in this respect, like a church: you must first be sinful to become a saint—otherwise you remain a plain, decent person with no chance of a career in the archives of God's memory. This is why, paradoxically, the more you want to free yourself from the museum, the more you become subjected in the most radical way to the logic of museum collecting, and vice versa.

Of course, this interpretation of the new, real, and living contradicts a certain deep-rooted conviction found in many texts of the earlier avant-garde—namely, that the way into life can be opened only by the destruction of the museum and by a radical, ecstatic deletion of the past, which stands between us and our present. This vision of the new is powerfully expressed, for example, in a short but important text by Kazimir Malevich: "On the Museum," from 1919. At that time the new Soviet government feared that the old Russian museums and art collections would be destroyed by civil war and the general collapse of state institutions and the economy, and the Communist Party responded by trying to save these collections. In his text, Malevich protested against this pro-museum policy of Soviet power by calling on the state to not intervene on behalf of the art collections because their destruction could open the path to true, living art. In particular, he wrote:

> Life knows what it is doing, and if it is striving to destroy one must not interfere, since by hindering we are blocking the path to a new conception of life that is born within us. In burning a corpse we obtain one gram of powder: accordingly thousands of graveyards could be accommodated on a single chemist's shelf. We can make a concession to conservatives by offering that they burn all past epochs, since they are dead, and set up one pharmacy.

Later, Malevich gives a concrete example of what he means:

> The aim (of this pharmacy) will be the same, even if people will examine the powder from Rubens and all his art—a mass of ideas will arise in people, and will be often more alive than actual representation (and take up less room).[1]

The example of Rubens is not accidental for Malevich; in many of his earlier manifestos, he states that it has become impossible in our time to paint "the fat ass of Venus" any more. Malevich also wrote in an earlier text about his famous *Black Square*—which became one of the most recognized symbols of the new in the art of that time—that there is no chance that "the sweet smile of Psyche emerges on my black square" and that it—the *Black Square*—"can never be used as a bed (mattress) for love-making."[2] Malevich hated the monotonous rituals of love-making at least as much as the monotonous museum collections. But most important is the conviction—underlying this statement of his—that a new, original, innovative art would be unacceptable for museum collections governed by the conventions of the past. In fact, the situation was the opposite in Malevich's time and, actually, had been so since the emergence of the museum as a modern institution at the end of the eighteenth century. Museum collecting is governed, in modernity, not by some well-established, definite, normative taste with a clear origin in the past. Rather, it is the idea of historical representation that compels the museum system to collect, in the first place, all those objects that are characteristic of certain historical epochs—including the contemporary epoch. This notion of historical representation has never been called into question—not even by quite recent postmodern writing which, in its turn, pretends to be historically new, truly contemporary and up-to-date. They go no further than asking, Who and what is *new enough* to represent our own time?

Only if the past is not collected, if the art of the past is not secured by the museum, does it make sense—and even become a kind a moral obligation—to remain faithful to the old, to follow traditions and resist the destructive work of time. Cultures without museums are the "cold cultures," as Levi-Strauss defined them, and these cultures try to keep their cultural identity intact by constantly reproducing the past. They do this because they feel the threat of oblivion, of a complete loss of historical memory. Yet if the past is collected and preserved in museums, the replication of old styles, forms, conventions, and traditions becomes unnecessary. Even more, the repetition of the old and traditional becomes a socially forbidden, or at least unrewarding, practice. The most general formula of modern art is not "Now I am free to do something new." Rather, it is that it is impossible to do the old anymore. As Malevich says, it had became impossible to paint the fat ass of Venus. But it became impossible only because of the existence of the museum. If Rubens' works really were burned, as Malevich suggested, it would in fact open the way for artists to paint the fat ass of Venus once again. The avant-garde strategy begins not with an opening to a greater freedom, but with the emergence of a new taboo—the "museum taboo," which forbids the repetition of the old because the old no longer disappears but remains on display.

The museum doesn't dictate what the new has to look like, it only shows what it must not look like, functioning like a demon of Socrates who told Socrates only what he must *not* do, but never what he must do. We can name this demonic voice, or presence, "the inner curator." Every modern artist has an inner curator who tells the artist what it is no longer possible to do, that is, what is no longer being collected. The museum gives us a rather clear definition of what it means for art to look real, alive, present—namely, it cannot look like already museographed, already collected art. Presence is not defined here solely by opposition to absence. To *be* present, art has also to *look* present. And this means it cannot look like the old, dead art of the past as it is presented in the museum.

We can even say that, under the conditions of the modern museum, the newness of newly produced art is not established post factum, as a result of comparison with old art. Rather, the comparison takes place before the emergence of the new artwork—and virtually produces this new artwork. The modern artwork is collected before it is even produced. The art of the avant-garde is the art of an elitist-thinking minority not because it expresses some specific bourgeois taste (as, for example, Bourdieu asserts), because, in a way, avant-garde art expresses no taste at all—no public taste, no personal taste, not even the taste of the artists themselves. Avant-garde art is elitist simply because it originates under a constraint to which the general public is not subjected. For the general public, all things—or at least most things—could be new because they are unknown, even if they are already collected in museums. This observation opens the way to making the central distinction necessary to achieve a better understanding of the phenomenon of the new—that between *new* and *other*, or between the new and the different.

Being new is, in fact, often understood as a combination of being different and being recently produced. We call a car a *new* car if this car is different from other cars, and at the same time if it is the latest, most recent model produced by the car industry. But as Søren Kierkegaard pointed out—especially in his *Philosophische Brocken*—being new is by no means the same as being different. Kierkegaard even rigorously opposes the notion of the new to the notion of difference, his main point being that a certain difference is recognized as such only because we already have the capability to recognize and identify this difference as difference. So no difference can ever be new—because if it were really new it could not be recognized as difference. To recognize means, always, to remember. But a recognized, remembered difference is obviously not a new difference.[3] Therefore there is, according to

Kierkegaard, no such thing as a new car. Even if a car is quite recent, the difference between this car and earlier produced cars is not one of being new, because this difference can be recognized by a spectator. This makes understandable why the notion of the new was somehow suppressed in art theoretical discourse of later decades, even if the notion kept its relevance for artistic practice. Such suppression is an effect of the preoccupation with Difference and Otherness in the context of structuralist and poststructuralist modes of thinking which have dominated recent cultural theory. But for Kierkegaard the new is a difference without difference, or a difference beyond difference—a difference that we are unable to recognize because it is not related to any pregiven structural code.

As an example of such difference, Kierkegaard uses the figure of Jesus Christ. Indeed, Kierkegaard states that the figure of Christ initially looked like that of every other ordinary human being at that historical time. In other words, an objective spectator at that time, confronted with the figure of Christ, could not find any visible, concrete difference between Christ and an ordinary human being—a visible difference that could suggest that Christ was not simply a man, but also the son of God. Thus, for Kierkegaard, Christianity is based on the impossibility of recognizing Christ as God—the impossibility of recognizing Christ as different. Further, this implies that Christ is *really* new and not merely different—and that Christianity is a manifestation of difference without difference, or, of difference *beyond* difference. Therefore, for Kierkegaard, the only medium for a possible emergence of the new is the ordinary, "nondifferent," identical—not the Other, but the Same. Yet the question arises, then, of how to deal with this difference beyond difference. How can the new manifest itself?

If we look more closely at the figure of Jesus Christ as described by Kierkegaard, it is striking that it appears to be quite similar to what we now call the "readymade." For Kierkegaard, the difference between God and man is not one that can be established objectively or described in visual terms. We put the figure of Christ into the context of the divine without recognizing Christ as divine—and that is what makes him genuinely new. But the same can be said of the readymades of Duchamp. Here we are also dealing with difference beyond difference—now understood as difference between the artwork and the ordinary, profane object. Accordingly, we can say that Duchamp's *Fountain* is a kind of Christ among things, and the art of the readymade a kind of Christianity of the art world. Christianity takes the figure of a human being and puts it, unchanged, in the context of religion, the Pantheon of the pagan gods. The museum—an art space or the whole art system—also functions as a place where difference beyond difference, between artwork and mere thing, can be produced or staged.

As I have mentioned, a new artwork cannot repeat the forms of old, traditional, already collected art. But today, to be really new, an artwork cannot even repeat the old differences between art objects and ordinary things. By means of repeating these differences, it is possible only to create a different artwork, not a new artwork. The new artwork looks really new and alive only if it resembles, in a certain sense, every other ordinary, profane thing, or every other ordinary product of popular culture. Only in this case can the new artwork function as a signifier for the world outside the museum walls. The new can be experienced as such only if it produces an effect of out-of-bounds infinity—if it opens an infinite view on reality outside of the museum. And this effect of infinity can be produced, or, better, staged, only inside the museum: in the context of reality itself we can experience the real only as finite because we ourselves are finite. The small, controllable space of the museum allows the spectator to imagine the world outside the museum's walls as splendid, infinite, ecstatic. This is, in fact, the primary function of the museum: to let us imagine what is outside the museum as infinite. New artworks function in the museum as symbolic windows opening onto a view of the infinite outside. But, of course, new artworks can fulfill this function only for a relatively short period of time before becoming no longer new but merely different, their distance from ordinary things having become, with time, all too obvious. The need then emerges to replace the old new with the new new, in order to restore the romantic feeling of the infinite real.

The museum is, in this respect, not so much a space for the representation of art history as a machine that produces and stages the new art of today—in other words, produces "today" as such. In this sense, the museum produces, for the first time, the effect of presence, of looking alive. Life looks truly alive only if we see it from the perspective of the museum, because, again, only in the museum are we able to produce new differences—differences beyond differences—differences that are emerging here and now. This possibility of producing new differences doesn't itself exist in reality, because in reality we find only old differences—differences that we can recognize. To produce new differences we need a space of culturally recognized and codified "nonreality." The difference between life and death is, in fact, of the same order as that between God and the ordinary human being, or between artwork and mere thing—it is a difference beyond difference, which can only be experienced, as I have said, in the museum or archive as a socially recognized space of "nonreal." Again, life today looks alive, and is alive, only when seen from the perspective of the archive, museum, library. In reality itself we are confronted only with dead differences—like the difference between a new and an old car.

Not too long ago it was widely expected that the readymade technique, together with the rise of photography and video art, would lead to the erosion and ultimate demise of the museum as it has established itself in modernity. It looked as though the closed space of the museum collection faced an imminent threat of inundation by the serial production of readymades, photographs, and media images that would lead to its eventual dissolution. To be sure, this prognosis owed its plausibility to a certain specific notion of the museum—that museum collections enjoy their exceptional, socially privileged status because they contain very special things, namely works of art, which are different from the normal, profane things of life. If museums were created to take in and harbor such special and wonderful things, then it indeed seems plausible that museums would face certain demise if this claim ever proved to be deceptive. And it is the very practices of readymades, photography, and video art that are said to provide clear proof that the traditional claims of museology and art history are illusory by making evident that the production of images is no mysterious process requiring an artist of genius.

This is what Douglas Crimp claimed in his well-known essay, "On the Museum's Ruins," with reference to Walter Benjamin: "Through reproductive technology, postmodernist art dispenses with the aura. The fiction of the creating subject gives way to the frank confiscation, quotation, excerptation, accumulation and repetition of already existing images. Notions of originality, authenticity and presence, essential to the ordered discourse of the museum, are undermined."[4] The new techniques of artistic production dissolve the museum's conceptual frameworks—constructed as they are on the fiction of subjective, individual creativity—bringing them into disarray through their reproductive practice and ultimately leading to the museum's ruin. And rightly so, it might be added, for the museum's conceptual frameworks are illusory: they suggest a representation of the historical, understood as a temporal epiphany of creative subjectivity, in a place where in fact there is nothing more than an incoherent jumble of artifacts, as Crimp asserts with reference to Foucault. Thus Crimp, like many other authors of his generation, regards any critique of the Romantic conception of art as a critique of art as institution, including the institution of the museum which is purported to legitimize itself primarily on the basis of this exaggerated and, at the same time, outmoded conception of art.

That the rhetoric of uniqueness—and difference—that legitimizes art by praising well-known masterpieces has long determined traditional art historical discourse is indisputable. It is nevertheless questionable whether this discourse in fact provides a decisive legitimization for the museological collecting of art, so that its critical analysis can at the same time function as a critique of the museum as institution. And, if the individual artwork can set itself apart from all other things by virtue of its artistic quality or, to put it in another way, as the manifestation of the creative genius of its author, would not the museum then be rendered completely superfluous? We can recognize and duly appreciate a masterful painting, if indeed such a thing exists, even—and most effectively so—in a thoroughly profane space.

However, the accelerated development we have witnessed in recent decades of the institution of the museum, above all of the museum of contemporary art, has paralleled the accelerated erasure of visible differences between artwork and profane object—an erasure systematically perpetrated by the avant-gardes of the twentieth century, most particularly since the 1960s. The less an artwork differs visually from a profane object, the more necessary it becomes to draw a clear distinction between the art context and the profane, everyday, nonmuseuological context of its occurrence. It is when an artwork looks like a "normal thing" that it requires the contextualization and protection of the museum. To be sure, the museum's safekeeping function is an important one also for traditional art that would stand out in an everyday environment, since it protects such art from physical destruction over time. As for the reception of this art, however, the museum is superfluous, if not detrimental: the contrast between the individual work and its everyday, profane environment—the contrast through which the work comes into its own—is for the most part lost in the museum. Conversely, the artwork that does not stand out with sufficient visual distinctness from its environment is truly perceivable only in the museum. The strategies of the artistic avant-garde, understood as the elimination of visual difference between artwork and profane thing lead directly, therefore, to the *building up* of museums, which secure this difference institutionally.

Far from subverting and delegitimizing the museum as institution, then, the critique of the emphatic conception of art in fact provides a theoretical foundation for the institutionalization and "musealization" of contemporary art. In the museum, ordinary objects are promised the distinction they do not enjoy in reality—the difference beyond difference. This promise is all the more valid and credible the less these objects "deserve" such a promise, that is, the less spectacular and extraordinary they are. The modern museum proclaims its new gospel not for the exclusive work of genius marked by aura, but rather for the insignificant, trivial, and everyday, which would otherwise soon drown in the reality outside the museum's walls. If the museum were ever actually to disintegrate, then the very opportunity for art to show the normal, the everyday, the trivial as new and truly alive would be lost. In order to assert itself successfully "in life," art must become different—unusual, surprising, exclusive—and history demonstrates that art can do this only by tapping into classical, mythological, and religious traditions and breaking its connection with the banality of everyday experience. The successful (and deservedly so) mass-cultural image production of our day concerns itself with alien attacks, myths of apocalypse and redemption, heroes endowed with superhuman powers, and so forth. All of this is certainly fascinating and instructive. Once in a while, though, one would like to be able to contemplate and enjoy something normal, something ordinary, something banal as well. In our culture, this wish can be gratified only in the museum. In life, on the other hand, only the extraordinary is presented to us as a possible object of our admiration.

But this also means that the new is still possible, because the museum is *still there* even after the alleged end of art history, of the subject, and so on. The relationship of the museum to what is outside is not primarily temporal, but spatial. And, indeed, innovation does not occur in time, but rather in space: on the other side of the physical boundaries between the museum collection and the outside world. We are able to cross these boundaries, literally and metaphorically, at any time, at very different points and in very different directions. And that means, further, that we can—and in fact must—dissociate the concept of the new from the concept of history, and the concept of innovation from its association with the linearity of historical time. The postmodern criticism of the notion of progress or of the utopias of modernity becomes irrelevant when artistic innovation is no longer thought of in terms of temporal linearity, but as the spatial relationship between the museum space and its outside. The new emerges not in historical life itself from some hidden source, and neither does it emerge as a promise of a hidden historical *telos*. The production of the new is merely a result of the shifting of the boundaries between collected items and noncollected items, the profane objects outside the collection, which is primarily a physical, material operation: some objects are brought into the museum system, while others are thrown out of the museum system and land, let us say, in the garbage. Such shifting produces again and again the effect of newness, openness, infinity, using signifiers that make art objects look different from those of the musealized past and identical with mere things and popular cultural images circulating in the space outside the museum. In this sense we can retain the concept of the new well beyond the alleged end of the art historical narrative through the production, as I have already mentioned, of new differences beyond all historically recognizable differences.

The materiality of the museum is a guarantee that the production of the new in art can transcend all ends of history, precisely because it demonstrates that the modern ideal of universal and transparent museum space (as a representation of universal art history) is unrealizable and purely ideological. The art of modernity has developed under the regulative idea of the universal museum representing the entire history of art and creating a universal, homogeneous space that allows the comparison of all possible artworks and the determination of their visual differences. This universalist vision was very well captured by André Malraux by his famous concept of "Musée imaginaire." Such a vision of a universal museum is Hegelian in its theoretical origin, as it embodies a notion of historical self-consciousness that is able to recognize all historically determined differences. And the logic of the relationship between art and the universal museum follows the logic of the Hegelian Absolute Spirit: the subject of knowledge and memory is motivated throughout the entire history of its dialectical development by the desire for the other, for the different, for the new—but at the end of this history it must discover and accept that otherness as such is produced by the movement of desire itself. And at this endpoint of history, the subject recognizes in the other its own image. So we can say that at the moment when the universal museum is understood as the actual origin of the other, because the other of the museum is by definition the object of desire for the museum collector or curator, the museum becomes, let us say, the Absolute Museum, and reaches the end of its possible history. Moreover, one can interpret the ready-made technique of Duchamp in Hegelian terms as an act of the self-reflection of the universal museum which puts an end to its further historical development.

So it is by no means accidental that the recent discourses proclaiming the end of art point to the advent of the readymade as the endpoint of art history. Arthur Danto's favorite example, when making his point that art reached the end of its history some time ago,[5] is that of Warhol's *Brillo Boxes*. And Thierry de Duve talks about "Kant after Duchamp," meaning the return of personal taste after the end of art history brought about by the readymade.[6] In fact, for Hegel himself, the end of art, as he argues in his lectures on aesthetics, takes place at a much earlier time: it coincides with the emergence of the new modern state which gives its own form, its own law, to the life of its citizens so that art loses its genuine form-giving function.[7] The Hegelian modern state codifies all visible and experiential differences—recognizes them, accepts them, and gives them their appropriate place within a general system of law. After such an act of political and judicial recognition of the other by modern law, art seems to lose its historical function, which was to manifest the otherness of the other, to give it a form, and to inscribe it in the system of historical representation. Thus at the moment at which law triumphs, art becomes impossible: The law already represents all the existing differences, making such a representation by means of art superfluous. Of course, it can be argued that some differences will always remain unrepresented or, at least, underrepresented, by the law, so that art retains at least some of its function of representing the uncodified other. But in this case, art fulfills only a secondary role of serving the law: the genuine role of art which consists, for Hegel, in being the mode by which differences originally manifest themselves and create forms is, in any case, passé under the effect of modern law.

But, as I said, Kierkegaard can show us, by implication, how an institution that has the mission to re-present differences can also create differences—beyond all preexisting differences. At this point I can formulate more precisely what this new difference is—this difference beyond difference—of which I spoke earlier. It is a difference not in form, but in time—namely, it is a difference in the life expectancy of individual things, as well as in their historical assignment. Recall the "new difference" as described by Kierkegaard: for him the difference between Christ and an ordinary human being of his time was not a difference in form which could be re-presented by art and law but a nonperceptible difference between the short time of ordinary human life and the eternity of divine existence. If I move a certain ordinary thing as a readymade from outside of the museum to its inner space, I don't change the form of this thing but I do change its life expectancy and assign to it a certain historical date. The artwork lives longer and keeps its original form longer in the museum than an ordinary object does in "reality." That is why an ordinary thing looks more "alive" and more "real" in the museum than in reality itself. If I see a certain ordinary thing in reality I immediately anticipate its death—as when it is broken and thrown away. A finite life expectancy is, in fact, the definition of ordinary life. So if I change the life expectancy of an ordinary thing, I change everything without, in a way, changing anything.

This nonperceptible difference in the life expectancy of a museum item and that of a "real thing" turns our imagination from the external images of things to the mechanisms of maintenance, restoration, and, generally, material support—the inner core of museum items. This issue of relative life expectancy also draws our attention to the social and political conditions under which these items are collected into the museum and thereby guaranteed longevity. At the same time, however, the museum's system of rules of conduct and taboos makes its support and protection of the object invisible and unexperienceable. This invisibility is irreducible. As is well known, modern art tried in all possible ways to make the inner, material side of the work transparent. But it is still only the surface of the artwork that we can see as museum spectators: behind this surface something remains forever concealed under the conditions of a museum visit. As a spectator in the museum, one always has to submit to restrictions which function fundamentally to keep the material substance of the artworks inaccessible and intact so that they may be exhibited "forever." We have here an interesting case of "the outside in the inside." The material support of the artwork is "in the museum" but at the same time it is not visualized—and not visualizable. The material support, or the medium bearer, as well as the entire system of museum conservation, must remain obscure, invisible, hidden from the museum spectator. In a certain sense, inside the museum's walls we are confronted with an even more radically inaccessible infinity than in the infinite world outside the museum's walls.

But if the material support of the musealized artwork cannot be made transparent it is nevertheless possible to explicitly thematize it as obscure, hidden, invisible. As an example of how such a strategy functions in the context of contemporary art, we may think of the work of two Swiss artists, Peter Fischli and David Weiss. For my present purposes a very brief description is sufficient: Fischli and Weiss exhibit objects that look very much like readymades—everyday objects as you see them everywhere in daily life.[8] In fact, these objects are not "real" readymades, but simulations: they are carved from polyurethane—a lightweight plastic material—but they are carved with such precision (a fine Swiss precision) that if you see them in a museum, in the context of an exhibition, you would have great difficulty distinguishing between the objects made by Fischli and Weiss and real readymades. If you saw these objects, let us say, in the atelier of Fischli and Weiss, you could take them in your hand and weigh them—an experience that would be impossible in a museum since it is forbidden to touch exhibited objects. To do so would be to immediately alert the alarm system, the museum personnel, and then the police. In this sense we can say that it is the police that, in the last instance, guarantee the opposition between art and non-art—the police who are not yet aware of the end of art history.

Fischli and Weiss demonstrate that readymades, while manifesting their form inside the museum space, are at the same time obscuring or concealing their own materiality. Nevertheless, this obscurity—the nonvisuality of the material support as such—is exhibited in the museum through the work of Fischli and Weiss, by way of their work's explicit evocation of the invisible difference between "real" and "simulated." The museum spectator is informed by the inscription accompanying the work that the objects exhibited by Fischli and Weiss are not "real" but "simulated" readymades. But at the same time the museum spectator cannot test this information because it relates to the hidden inner core, the material support of the exhibited items—and not to their visible form. This means that the newly introduced difference between "real" and "simulated" does not represent any already established visual differences between things on the level of their form. The material support cannot be revealed in the individual artwork—even if many artists and theoreticians of the historical avant-garde wanted it to be revealed. Rather, this difference can only be explicitly thematized in the museum as obscure and unrepresentable. By simulating the readymade technique, Fischli and Weiss direct our attention to the material support without revealing it, without making it visible, without re-presenting it. The difference between "real" and "simulated" cannot be "recognized," only produced, because every object in the world can be seen at the same time as both "real" and as "simulated." We can produce the difference between real and simulated by putting a certain thing or image under the suspicion of being not "real" but merely "simulated." And to put a certain ordinary thing into the museum context means precisely to put the medium bearer, the material support, the material conditions of existence of this thing, under permanent suspicion. The work of Fischli and Weiss demonstrates that there is an obscure infinity in the museum itself—it is the infinite doubt, the infinite suspicion of all exhibited things being simulated, being fakes, having a material core other than that suggested by their external form. And this also means that it is not possible to transfer "the entirety of visible reality" into the museum—even in the imagination. Neither is it possible to fulfill the old Nietzschean dream of aestheticizing the world in its totality, in order to achieve the identification of reality with the museum. The museum produces its own obscurities, invisibilities, differences; it produces its own concealed outside on the inside. And the museum can only create the athmosphere of suspicion, uncertainty, and angst in respect to the hidden support of the artworks displayed in the museum which, while guaranteeing their longevity, at the same time endangers their authenticity.

The artificial longevity guaranteed to things collected and put inside a museum is *always* a simulation; this longevity can only be achieved through a technical manipulation of the hidden material core of the exhibited thing to secure its durability: Every conservation is a technical manipulation which is also necessarily a simulation. Yet, such artificial longevity of an artwork can only be relative. The time comes when every artwork dies, is broken up, dissolved, deconstructed—not necessarily theoretically, but on the material level. The Hegelian vision of the universal museum is one in which corporeal eternity is substituted for the eternity of the soul in the memory of God. But such a corporeal eternity is, of course, an illusion. The museum itself is a temporal thing—even if the artworks collected in the museum are removed from the dangers of everyday existence and general exchange with their preservation as its goal. This preservation cannot succeed, or it can succeed only temporarily. Art objects are destroyed regularly by wars, catastrophes, accidents, time. This material fate, this irreducible temporality of art objects as material things, puts a limit on every possible art history—but a limit that functions at the same time as the opposite of the end of history. On a purely material level, the art context changes permanently in a way that we cannot entirely control, reflect, or predict, so that this material change always comes to us as a surprise. Historical self-reflection is dependent on the hidden, unreflectable materiality of the museum's objects. And precisely because the material fate of art is irreducible and unreflectable, the history of art must be revisited, reconsidered, and rewritten always anew.

Even if the material existence of an individual artwork is for a certain time guaranteed, the status of this artwork as artwork depends always on the context of its presentation in a museum collection. But it is extremely difficult—actually impossible—to stabilize this context over a long period of time. This is, perhaps, the true paradox of the museum: the museum collection serves the preservation of artifacts, but this collection itself is always extremely unstable, constantly changing and in flux. Collecting is an event in time par excellence—even while it is an attempt to escape time. The museum exhibition flows permanently: it is not only growing or progressing, but it is changing itself in many different ways. Consequently, the framework for distinguishing between the old and the new, and for ascribing to things the status of an artwork, is changing all the time too. Artists such as Mike Bidlo or Shirley Levine demonstrate, for example—through the technique of appropriation—the possibility of shifting the historical assignment of given art forms by changing their material support. The copying or repetition of well-known artworks brings the whole order of historical memory into disarray. It is impossible for an average spectator to distinguish between, say, the original Picasso work and the Picasso work appropriated by Mike Bidlo. So here, as in the case of Duchamp's readymade, or the simulated readymades of

Fischli and Weiss, we are confronted with a nonvisual difference and, in this sense, a newly produced difference—the difference between a work of Picasso and a copy of this work produced by Bidlo. This difference again can be staged only within the museum—within a certain order of historical representation.

In this way, by placing already existing artworks into new contexts, changes in the display of an artwork can effect a difference in its reception, without there having been any change in the artwork's visual form. In recent times, the status of the museum as the site of a permanent collection is gradually shifting to one of the museum as theater for large-scale traveling exhibitions organized by international curators, and large-scale installations created by individual artists. Every large exhibition or installation of this kind is made with the intention of designing a new order of historical memories, of proposing new criteria for collecting by reconstructing history. These traveling exhibitions and installations are temporal museums that openly display their temporality. The difference between traditional modernist and contemporary art strategies is, therefore, relatively easy to describe. In the modernist tradition, the art context was regarded as stable—it was the idealized context of the universal museum. Innovation consisted in putting a new form, a new thing, into this stable context. In our time, the context is seen as changing and unstable. So the strategy of contemporary art consists in creating a specific context that can make a certain form or thing look other, new and interesting—even if this form has already been collected. Traditional art worked on the level of form. Contemporary art works on the level of context, framework, background, or of a new theoretical interpretation. But the goal is the same: to create a contrast between form and historical background, to make the form look other and new.

So, Fischli and Weiss may now exhibit readymades that look completely familiar to the contemporary viewer. Their difference from standard readymades, as I said, cannot be seen, because the inner materiality of the works cannot be seen. It can only be told: we have to listen to a story, to a history of making these pseudo-readymades to grasp the difference, or, better, to imagine the difference. In fact, it is not even necessary for these works of Fischli and Weiss to be actually "made"; it is enough to tell the story that enables us to look at the "models" for these works in a different way. Ever-changing museum presentations compel us to imagine the Heraclitean flux that deconstructs all identities and undermines all historical orders and taxonomies, ultimately destroying all the archives from within. But such a Heraclitean vision is possible only inside the museum, inside the archives, because only there are the archival orders, identities, and taxonomies established to a degree that allows us to imagine their possible destruction as something sublime. Such a sublime vision is impossible in the context of "reality" itself, which offers us perceptual differences but not differences in respect to the historical order. Also, through continuous change in its exhibitions, the museum can present its hidden, obscure materiality—without revealing it.

It is no accident that we can now watch the growing success of such narrative art forms as video and cinema installations in the context of the museum. Video installations bring the "great night" into the museum—it may be their most important function. The museum space loses its own "institutional" light, which traditionally functioned as a symbolic property of the viewer, the collector, the curator. The museum becomes obscure, dark, and dependent on the light emanating from the video image, that is, from the hidden core of the artwork, from the electrical and computer technology hidden within its form. It is not the art object that is exhibited in the museum, which should be enlightened, examined, and judged by the museum, as in earlier times; rather this technologically produced image brings its own light into the darkness of the museum space—and only for a certain period of time. It is also interesting to note that if the spectator tries to intrude on the inner, material core of the video installation while the installation is "working," he will be electrocuted, which is even more effective than an intervention by the police. Similarly, an unwanted intruder into the forbidden, inner space of a Greek temple was supposed to be struck by the lightning bolt of Zeus.

And more than that: not only control over the light, but also control over the time necessary for contemplation is passed from the visitor to the artwork. In the classical museum, the visitor exercises almost complete control over the duration of contemplation. He or she can interrupt contemplation at any time, return, and go away again. The picture stays where it is, making no attempt to flee the viewer's gaze. With moving pictures this is no longer the case—they escape the viewer's control. When we turn away from a video, we usually miss something. Now the museum—earlier, a place of complete visibility—becomes a place where we cannot compensate for a missed opportunity to contemplate—where we cannot return to the same place to watch the same thing we saw before. And even more so than in so-called real life, because under the standard conditions of an exhibition visit, a spectator is in most cases physically unable to watch all the videos on display, their cumulative length exceeding the time of a museum visit. In this way, the advent of video and cinema installation in the museum demonstrates the finiteness of time and also reveals the distance to the light source that remains concealed under the normal conditions of video and film circulation in our popular culture. Or better: the film becomes uncertain, invisible, obscure to the spectator owing to its placement in the museum—the length of the film being, as a rule, longer than the average time of a museum visit. Here again a new difference in film reception emerges as a result of substituting the museum for an ordinary film theater.

To summarize the point I have been trying to make: The modern museum is capable of introducing a new difference between collected and noncollected things. This difference is new because it does not re-present any already existing visual differences. The choice of the objects for musealization is interesting and relevant for us only if it does not merely recognize and restate existing differences, but presents itself as unfounded, unexplainable, illegitimate. Such a choice opens for a spectator a view on the infinity of the world. And more than that: By introducing such a new difference, the museum shifts the attention of the spectator from the visual form of things to their hidden material support and to their life expectancy. The new functions here not as a re-presentation of the other and also not as a next step in a progressive clarification of the obscure, but rather as a new reminder that the obscure remains obscure, that the difference between real and simulated remains ambiguous, that the longevity of things is always endangered, that infinite doubt about the inner nature of things is insurmountable. Or, to put it another way: The museum provides the possibility of introducing the sublime into the banal. In the Bible, we can find the famous statement that there is nothing new under the sun. That is, of course, true. But there is no sun inside the museum. And that is probably why the museum always was—and remains—the only possible site of innovation.

On the Curatorship

The work of the curator consists of placing artworks in the exhibition space. This is what differentiates the curator from the artist, as the artist has the privilege to exhibit objects which have not already been elevated to the status of artworks. In this case they gain this status precisely through being placed in the exhibition space. Duchamp, in exhibiting the urinal, is not a curator but an artist, because as a result of his decision to present the urinal in the framework of an exhibition, this urinal has become a work of art. This opportunity is denied to the curator. He can of course exhibit a urinal, but only if it is Duchamp's urinal—that is, a urinal that has already obtained art status. The curator can easily exhibit an unsigned urinal, one without art status, but it will merely be regarded as an example of a certain period of European design, serve as "contextualization" for exhibited artworks, or fulfill some other subordinate function. In no way can this urinal obtain art status—and after the end of the exhibition it will return not to the museum, but back to where it came from. The curator may exhibit, but he doesn't have the magical ability to transform nonart into art through the act of display. That power, according to current cultural conventions, belongs to the artist alone.

It hasn't been always so. Originally, art became art through decisions of curators rather than artists. The first art museums came into existence at the turn of the nineteenth century, and became established over the course of the nineteenth century as a consequence of revolutions, wars, imperial conquest, and pillage of non-European cultures. All kinds of "beautiful" functional objects—previously used for various religious rituals, decorating the rooms of those in power, or manifesting private wealth—were collected and put on display as works of art—that is, as defunctionalized, autonomous objects of pure contemplation. The curators administering these museums "created" art through iconoclastic acts directed against traditional icons of religion or power, by reducing these icons to mere artworks. Art was originally "just" art. This perception of it as such is situated within the tradition of the European Enlightenment, which conceived of all religious icons as "profane, secularized things"—and art solely as beautiful objects, as mere artworks. The question is then, why have curators lost the power to create art through the act of its exhibition, and why has this power passed over to artists?

The answer is obvious: In exhibiting a urinal, Duchamp does not devalue a sacred icon, as the museum curators had done; he rather upgrades a mass-produced object to an artwork. In this way the exhibition's role in the symbolic economy has changed. Sacred objects were once devalued to produce art; today, in contrast, profane objects are valorized to become art. What was originally iconoclasm has turned into iconophilia. But this shift in the symbolic economy had already been put in motion by the curators and art critics of the nineteenth century.

Every exhibition tells a story, by directing the viewer through the exhibition in a particular order; the exhibition space is always a narrative space. The traditional art museum told the story of art's emergence and subsequent victory. Individual artworks chronicled this story—and in doing so they lost their old religious or representative significance and gained new meaning. Once the museum emerged as the new place of worship, artists began to work specifically for the museum: Historically significant objects no longer needed to be devalued in order to serve as art. Instead, brand new, profane objects signed up to be recognized as artworks because they allegedly embodied artistic value. These objects didn't have a prehistory; they had never been legitimized by religion or power. At most they could be regarded as signs of a "simple, everyday life" with indeterminate value. Thus their inscription into art history meant valorization for these objects, not devaluation. And so museums were transformed from places of enlightenment-inspired iconoclasm into places of a romantic iconophilia. Exhibiting an object as art no longer signified its profanation, but its consecration. Duchamp simply took this turn to its final conclusion when he laid bare the iconophilic mechanism of glorification of mere things by labeling them works of art.

Over the years modern artists began to assert the total autonomy of art—and not just from its sacred prehistory, but from art history as well—because every integration of an image into a story, every appropriation of it as illustration for a particular narrative, is iconoclastic, even if the story is that of a triumph of this image, its transfiguration, or its glorification. According to tradition of modern art, an image must speak for itself; it must immediately convince the spectator, standing in silent contemplation, of its own value. The conditions in which the work is exhibited should be reduced to white walls and good lighting. Theoretical and narrative discourse is a distraction, and must stop. Even affirmative discourse and favorable display were regarded as distorting the message of the artwork itself. As a result: Even after Duchamp the act of exhibiting any object as an artwork remained ambivalent, that is, partially iconophile, partially iconoclastic.

The curator can't but place, contextualize, and narrativize works of art—which necessarily leads to their relativization. Thus modern artists began to condemn curators, because the figure of the curator was perceived as the embodiment of the dark, dangerous, iconoclastic side of the exhibiting practice, as the destructive doppelgänger of the artist who creates art by exhibiting it: the museums were regularly compared to graveyards, and curators to undertakers. With these insults (disguised as institutional critique) artists won the general public over to their side, because the general public didn't know all the art history; it didn't even want to hear it. The public wishes to be confronted directly with individual artworks and exposed to their unmediated impact. The general public steadfastly believes in the autonomous meaning of the individual artwork, which is supposedly being manifested in front of its eyes. The curator's every mediation is suspect: he is seen as someone standing between the artwork and its viewer, insidiously manipulating the viewer's perception with the intent of disempowering the public. This is why, for the general public, the art market is more enjoyable than any museum. Artworks circulating on the market are singled out, decontextualized, uncurated—so that they have the apparently unadulterated chance to demonstrate their inherent value. Consequently the art market is an extreme example of what Marx termed commodity fetishism, meaning a belief in the inherent value of an object, in value being one of its intrinsic qualities. Thus began a time of degradation and distress for curators—the time of modern art. Curators have managed their degradation surprisingly well, though, by successfully internalizing it.

Even today we hear from many curators that they are working toward a single objective, that of making individual artworks appear in the most favorable light. Or to put it differently, the best curating is nil-curating, non-curating. From this perspective, the solution seems to be to leave the artwork alone, enabling the viewer to confront it directly. However, not even the renowned white cube is always good enough for this purpose. The viewer is often advised to completely abstract himself from the work's spatial surroundings, and to immerse herself fully in self- and world-denying contemplation. Under these conditions alone—beyond any kind of curating, that is—can one's encounter with an artwork be regarded as authentic and genuinely successful. That such contemplation cannot go ahead without the artwork's being exhibited, however, remains an indisputable fact. Giorgio Agamben writes that "the image is a being, that in its essence is appearance, visibility, or semblance."[1] But this definition of artwork's essence does not suffice to guarantee the visibility of a concrete artwork. A work of art cannot in fact present itself by virtue of its own definition and force the viewer into contemplation; it lacks the necessary vitality, energy, and health. Artworks seem to be genuinely sick and helpless—the spectator has to be led to the artwork, as hospital workers might take a visitor to see a bedridden patient. It is in fact no coincidence that the word "curator" is etymologically related to "cure." Curating is curing. The process of curating cures the image's powerlessness, its incapacity to present itself. The artwork needs external help, it needs an exhibition and curator to become visible. The medicine that makes the sick image appear healthy—makes the image literally appear, and do so in the best light—is the exhibition. In this respect, since iconophilia is dependent on the image appearing healthy and strong, the curatorial practice is, to a certain degree, the servant of iconophilia.

But at the same time, curatorial practice undermines iconophilia, for its medical artifice cannot remain entirely concealed from the viewer. In this respect, curating remains unintentionally iconoclastic even as it is programmatically iconophile. Indeed, curating acts as a supplement or a "pharmacon" (in Derrida's usage),[2] in that it cures the image even as it makes it unwell. Like art in general, curating cannot escape being simultaneously iconophile and iconoclast. Yet this statement points to the question: Which is the right kind of curatorial practice? Since curatorial practice can never entirely conceal itself, the main objective of curating must be to visualize itself, by making its practice explicitly visible. The will to visualization is in fact what constitutes and drives art. Since it takes place within the context of art, curatorial practice cannot elude the logic of visibility.

The visualization of curating demands a simultaneous mobilization of its iconoclastic potential. Contemporary iconoclasm, of course, can and should be aimed primarily not at religious icons but at art itself. By placing an artwork in a controlled environment, in the context of other carefully chosen objects, and above all involving it in a specific narrative, the curator is making an iconoclastic gesture. If this gesture is made sufficiently explicit, curating returns to its secular beginnings, withstanding the transformation of art into art-as-religion, and becomes an expression of art-atheism. The fetishization of art is taking place outside of the museum, which is to say outside of the zone in which the curator has traditionally exercised authority. Artworks now become iconic not as a result of their display in the museum but by their circulation in the art market and in the mass media. Under these circumstances, the curating of an artwork signifies its return to history, the transformation of the autonomous artwork back into an illustration—an illustration whose value is not contained within itself but is extrinsic, attached to it by a historical narrative.

Orhan Pamuk's novel *My Name Is Red* features a group of artists searching for a place for art within an iconoclastic culture, namely that of sixteenth-century Islamic Turkey. The artists are illustrators commissioned by those in power to ornament their books with exquisite miniature drawings; subsequently these books are placed in governmental or private collections. Not only are these artists increasingly persecuted by radical Islamic (iconoclastic) adversaries who want to ban all images; they are also in competition with the Occidental painters of the Renaissance, primarily Venetians, who openly affirm their own iconophilia. Yet the novel's heroes can't share this iconophilia, because they don't believe in the autonomy of images. And so they try to find a way to take a consistently honest iconoclastic stance, without abandoning the terrain of art. A Turkish sultan, whose theory of art would actually serve as good advice for contemporary curatorial practice, shows them the way:

> an illustration that does not complement a story, in the end, will become but a false idol. Since we cannot possibly believe in the absent story, we will naturally begin to believe in the picture itself. This would be no different than the worship of the idols in the Kaaba that went on before Our Prophet, peace and blessings be upon him, had them destroyed. . . . If I believed, heaven forbid, the way these infidels do, that the Prophet Jesus was also the Lord God himself, . . . only then might I accept the depiction of mankind in full detail and exhibit such images.

> You do understand that, eventually, we would then unthinkingly begin worshipping any picture that is hung on the wall, don't you?[3]

Strong iconoclastic tendencies and currents were naturally to be found in the Christian Occident as well—twentieth-century modern art in particular. Indeed, most modern art was created through iconoclasm. As a matter of fact, the avant-garde staged a martyrdom of the image, which replaced the Christian image of martyrdom. The avant-garde put traditional painting through all sorts of torture, which recall first and foremost the torture to which the saints were subjected as depicted in paintings in the Middle Ages. Thus the image is—symbolically and literally—sawed, cut, fragmented, drilled, pierced, dragged through the dirt, and left to the mercy of ridicule. No coincidence, then, that the historical avant-garde consistently employed the language of iconoclasm: avant-garde artists speak of demolishing traditions, breaking with conventions, destroying their artistic heritage, and annihilating old values. The iconoclastic gesture is instituted here as an artistic method, less for the annihilation of old icons than for the production of new images—or, if you prefer, new icons and new idols. Our iconographic imagination, which has long been honed by the Christian tradition, does not hesitate to recognize victory in the image of defeat as depicted by the image of Christ on the cross. In fact, here the defeat is a victory from the start. Modern art has benefited significantly from the adoption of iconoclasm as a mode of production.

Indeed, throughout the era of modernism, whenever an iconoclastic image been produced, hung on the wall, or presented in an exhibition space, it has become an idol. The reason is clear: modern art has struggled particularly hard against the image's illustrative use and its narrative function. The result of this struggle illustrates the sultan's premonition. Modern art wanted to purify the image of everything exterior to it, to render the image autonomous and self-sufficient—but in so doing only affirmed the dominant iconophilia. Thus iconoclasm has become subordinate to iconophilia: the symbolic martyrdom of the image only strengthens our belief in it.

The subtler iconoclastic strategy proposed by the sultan—turning the image back into an illustration—is actually much more effective. We have known at least since Magritte that when we look at an image of a pipe, we are regarding not a real pipe but one that has been re-presented. The pipe as such isn't there, it isn't present; instead, it is depicted as being absent. In spite of this knowledge we are still inclined to believe that when we look at an artwork, we directly and instantaneously confront "art." We see artworks as incarnating art. The famous distinction between art and non-art is generally understood as a distinction between objects inhabited and animated by art and those from which art is absent. This is how works of art become art's idols, that is, analogously to religious images, which are also believed to be inhabited or animated by gods.

On the other hand, to practice art-atheism would be to understand artworks not as incarnations, but as mere documents, illustrations, or signifiers of art. While they may refer to art, they are nevertheless not themselves art. To a greater or lesser extent this strategy has been pursued by many artists since the 1960s. Artistic projects, performances, and actions have regularly been documented, and by means of this documentation represented in exhibition spaces and museums. Such documentation, however, merely refers to art without itself being art. This type of documentation is often presented in the framework of an art installation for the purpose of narrating a certain project or action. Traditionally executed paintings, art objects, photographs, or videos can also be implemented in the framework of such installations. In this case, admittedly, artworks lose their previous status as art. Instead they become documents, illustrations of the story told by the installation. One could say that today's art audience increasingly encounters art *documentation*, which provides information about the artwork itself, be it art project or art action, but which in doing so only confirms the absence of the artwork.

But even if illustrativity and narrativity have managed to find their way into the halls of art, this entry by no means signifies the automatic triumph of art-atheism. Even if the artist loses faith, he or she doesn't thereby lose the magical ability to transform mere things into art, just as a Catholic priest's loss of faith doesn't render the rituals he performs ineffective. Meanwhile the installation itself has been blessed with art status: installation has become accepted as an art form and increasingly assumes a leading role in contemporary art. So even though the individual images and objects lose their autonomous status, the entire installation gains it back. When Marcel Broodthaers presented his *Musée d'Art Moderne, Département des Aigles* at the Kunsthalle in Düsseldorf in 1973, he placed the label "This is not a work of art" next to each of the presented objects in the installation. The entire installation, though, is legitimately considered to be an artwork.

Here the figure of the independent curator, increasingly central to contemporary art, comes into play. When it comes down to it, the independent curator does everything the contemporary artist does. The independent curator travels the world and organizes exhibitions that are comparable to artistic installations—comparable because they are the results of individual curatorial projects, decisions, and actions. The artworks presented in these exhibitions/installations take on the role of documentation of a curatorial project. Yet such curatorial projects are in no way iconophilic; they do not aim to glorify the image's autonomous value.

"Utopia Station" is a good example—curated by Molly Nesbit, Hans-Ulrich Obrist, and Rirkrit Tiravanija, this exhibition was presented at the Fiftieth Venice Biennale in 2003. Critical and public discussion of the project stressed the issues of whether the concept of utopia is still relevant; whether what was put forward as a utopian vision by the curators could really be regarded as such; and so on. Yet the fact that a curatorial project that was clearly iconoclastic could be presented at one of the oldest international art exhibitions seems to me to be far more important than the above considerations. It was iconoclastic because it employed artworks as illustrations, as documents of the search for a social utopia, without emphasizing their autonomous value. It subscribed to the radical iconoclastic approach of the classical Russian avant-garde, which considered art to be documentation of the search for the "new man" and a "new life." Most important, though, "Utopia Station" was a curatorial and not an artistic project. This meant that the iconoclastic gesture could not be accompanied—and thus invalidated—by the attribution of artistic value. Nevertheless, it can still be assumed that in this case the concept of utopia was abused, because it was aestheticized and situated in an elitist art context. And it can be equally said that art was abused as well: it served as an illustration for the curators' vision of utopia. Thus in both cases the spectator has to confront an abuse—be it an abuse of art or by art. Here, though, abuse is just another word for iconoclasm.

The independent curator is a radically secularized artist. He is an artist because he does everything artists do. But he is an artist who has lost the artist's aura, who no longer has magical transformative powers at his disposal, who cannot endow objects with artistic status. He doesn't use objects—art objects included—for art's sake, but rather abuses them, makes them profane. Yet it is precisely this that makes the figure of the independent curator so attractive and so essential to the art of today. The contemporary curator is the heir apparent to the modern artist, although he doesn't suffer from his predecessor's magical abnormalities. He is an artist, but he is atheistic and "normal" through and through. The curator is an agent of art's profanation, its secularization, its abuse. It can of course be stated that the independent curator, as the museum curator before him, cannot but depend on the art market—even lay the groundwork for it. An artwork's value increases when it is presented in a museum, or through its frequent appearance in the diverse temporary exhibitions organized by independent curators—and so, as before, the dominant iconophilia prevails. This iconophilia can be held to be understood and acknowledged—or not.

The market value of an artwork doesn't correspond exactly to its narrative or its historical value. The traditional "museum value" of an artwork is never the same as its value on the art market. A work of art can please, impress, excite the desire to possess it—all this while having no specific historical relevance and, therefore, remaining irrelevant to the museum's narrative. And conversely: many artworks may seem incomprehensible, boring, and depressing to the general public but are given a place in the museum, because they are "historically new" or at the very least "relevant" to a particular period, and therefore can be put to the task of illustrating a certain kind of art history. The widespread opinion that an artwork in a museum is "dead" can be understood as meaning that it loses its status as an idol there; pagan idols were venerated for being "alive." The museum's iconoclastic gesture consists precisely of transforming "living" idols into "dead" illustrations of art history. It can therefore be said that the traditional museum curator has always subjected images to the same double abuse as the independent curator. On the one hand, images in the museum are aestheticized and transformed into art; on the other, they are downgraded to illustrations of art history and thereby dispossessed of their art status.

This double abuse of images, this doubled iconoclastic gesture, is only recently being made explicit, because instead of narrating the canon of art history, independent curators are beginning to tell each other their own contradictory stories. In addition, these stories are being told by means of temporary exhibitions (which carry their own time limitations), and recorded by incomplete and frequently even incomprehensible documentation. The exhibition catalog for a curatorial project that already presents a double abuse can only produce a further abuse. But nevertheless, artworks become visible only as a result of this multiple abuse. Images don't emerge into the clearing of Being on their own accord, where their original visibility is then muddied by the "art business," as Heidegger describes it in *The Origin of the Work of Art*. It is far more that this very abuse makes them visible.

Art in the Age of Biopolitics: From Artwork to Art Documentation

In recent decades, it has become increasingly evident that the art world has shifted its interest away from the artwork and toward art documentation. This shift is particularly symptomatic of a broader transformation that art is undergoing today, and for that reason it deserves a detailed analysis.

The artwork as traditionally understood is something that embodies art in itself, that makes it immediately present and visible. When we go to an exhibition, we usually assume that what we will see there—whether paintings, sculptures, drawings, photographs, videos, readymades, or installations—*is* art. Artworks can, of course, refer in one way or another to something other than themselves—say, to objects in reality or to specific political subjects—but they cannot refer to art, because they *are* art. But this traditional assumption about what we find at an exhibition or museum is proving more and more misleading. Increasingly, in art spaces today we are confronted not just with artworks but with art documentation. The latter can also take the form of paintings, drawings, photographs, videos, texts, and installations—that is to say, all the same forms and media in which art is traditionally presented—but in the case of art documentation these media do not present art but merely document it. Art documentation is by definition *not* art; it merely *refers* to art, and in precisely this way it makes it clear that art, in this case, is no longer present and immediately visible but rather absent and hidden.

Art documentation refers to art in at least two different ways. It may refer to performances, temporary installations, or happenings, which are documented in the same ways as theatrical performances. In such cases, one might say that these are art events that were present and visible at a particular time, and that the documentation that is exhibited later is intended merely as a way of recollecting them. Whether such recollecting is really possible is, of course, an open question. Since the advent of deconstruction, if not before, we have been aware that any claim that past events can be recalled in this straightforward way must, at the very least, be considered problematic.

Meanwhile, however, more and more art documentation is being produced and exhibited that does not claim to make present any past art event. Examples include complex and varied artistic interventions in daily life, lengthy and complicated processes of discussion and analysis, the creation of unusual living circumstances, artistic exploration into the reception of art in various cultures and milieus, and politically motivated artistic actions. None of these artistic activities can be presented except by means of art documentation, since from the very beginning these activities do not serve to produce an artwork in which art as such could manifest itself. Consequently, such art does not appear in object form—is not a product or result of a "creative" activity. Rather, the art is itself this activity, is the practice of art as such. Correspondingly, art documentation is neither the making present of a past art event nor the promise of a coming artwork, but rather is the only possible form of reference to an artistic activity that cannot be represented in any other way.

Nevertheless, to categorize art documentation as "simple" artwork would be to misunderstand it by overlooking its originality, its identifying feature, which is precisely that it documents art rather than presenting it. For those who devote themselves to the production of art documentation rather than artworks, art is identical to life, because life is essentially a pure activity that has no end result. The presentation of any such end result—in the form of an artwork, say—would imply an understanding of life as a merely functional process whose own duration is negated and extinguished by the creation of the end product—which is equivalent to death. It is no coincidence that museums are traditionally compared to cemeteries: by presenting art as the end result of life, they obliterate life once and for all. Art documentation, by contrast, marks the attempt to use artistic media within art spaces to refer to life itself, that is, to a pure activity, to pure practice, to an artistic life, as it were, without presenting it directly. Art becomes a life form, whereas the artwork becomes non-art, a mere documentation of this life form. One could also say that art becomes biopolitical, because it begins to use artistic means to produce and document life as a pure activity. Indeed, art documentation as an art form could only develop under the conditions of today's biopolitical age, in which life itself has become the object of technical and artistic intervention. In this way, one is again confronted with the question of the relationship between art and life—and indeed in a completely new context, defined by the aspiration of today's art to become life itself, not merely to depict life or to offer it art products.

Traditionally, art was divided into pure, contemplative, "fine" art and applied art—that is, design. The former was concerned not with reality but with images of reality. Applied art built and composed the things of reality themselves. In this respect, art resembles science, which can also be divided into a theoretical and an applied version. The difference between fine art and theoretical science, however, is that science has wanted to make the images of reality that it creates as transparent as possible, in order to judge reality itself on the basis of these images, whereas art, taking another path, has taken as its theme its own materiality and lack of clarity, the obscurity and, there-fore, autonomy of images and the resulting inability of these images ade-quately to reproduce reality. Artistic images—from the "fantastic," the "unrealistic," by way of the Surrealistic and on up to the abstract—are intended to thematize the gap between art and reality. And even media that are usually thought of as reproducing reality faithfully—such as photography and film—are also used in the context of art in a way that seeks to undermine any faith in reproduction's ability to be faithful to reality. "Pure" art thus established itself on the level of the signifier. That to which the signifier refers—reality, meaning, the signified—has, by contrast, traditionally been interpreted as belonging to life and thus as removed from the sphere in which art is valid. Nor can it be said of applied art, however, that it concerns itself with life. Even if our environment is largely shaped by applied arts such as architecture, urban planning, product design, advertising, and fashion, it is still left to life to find the best way to deal with all these designed products. Life itself as pure activity, as pure duration, is thus fundamentally inaccessible to the traditional arts, which remain oriented toward products or results in one form or another.

In our age of biopolitics, however, the situation is changing, for the principal concern of this kind of politics is the lifespan itself. Biopolitics is often confused with scientific and technical strategies of genetic manipulation that, at least potentially, aim at reforming the individual living body. These strategies themselves, however, are still a matter of design—albeit that of a living organism. The real achievement of biopolitical technologies lies more in the shaping of the lifespan itself—in the shaping of life as a pure activity that occurs in time. From begetting and lifelong medical care by way of the regulation of the relationship between work time and free time up to death as supervised, or even brought about by, medical care, the lifetime of a person today is constantly being shaped and artificially improved. Many authors, from Michel Foucault and Giorgio Agamben to Antonio Negri and Michael Hardt, have written along these lines about biopolitics as the true realm in which political will and technology's power to shape things are manifested today. That is to say, if life is no longer understood as a natural event, as fate, as Fortuna, but rather as time artificially produced and fashioned, then life is automatically politicized, since the technical and artistic decisions with respect to the shaping of the lifespan are always political decisions as well. The art that is made under these new conditions of biopolitics—under the conditions of an artificially fashioned lifespan—cannot help but take this artificiality as its explicit theme. Now, however, time, duration, and thus life as well cannot be presented directly but only documented. The dominant medium of modern biopolitics is thus bureaucratic and technological documentation, which includes planning, decrees, fact-finding reports, statistical inquiries, and project plans. It is no coincidence that art also uses the same medium of documentation when it wants to refer to itself as life.

Indeed, one feature of modern technology is that we are no longer able by visual means alone to make a firm distinction between the natural or organic and the artificial or technologically produced. This is demonstrated by genetically modified food, but also by the numerous discussions—especially intense these days—about the criteria for deciding when life begins and when it ends. To put it another way: How does one distinguish between a technologically facilitated beginning of life, such as artificial insemination, for example, and a "natural" continuation of that life, or distinguish that natural continuation, in turn, from an equally technology-dependent means of extending life beyond a "natural" death? The longer these discussions go on, the less the participants are able to agree on where precisely the line between life and death can be drawn. Almost all recent sci-fi films have as a major theme this inability to distinguish between the natural and the artificial: the surface of a living being can conceal a machine; conversely, the surface of a machine can conceal a living being—an alien, for example.[1] The difference between a genuinely living creature and its artificial substitute is taken to be merely a product of the imagination, a supposition or suspicion that can be neither confirmed nor refuted by observation. But if the living thing can be reproduced and replaced at will, then it loses its unique, unrepeatable inscription in time—its unique, unrepeatable lifespan, which is ultimately what makes the living thing a living thing. And that is precisely the point at which the documentation becomes indispensable, producing the life of the living thing as such: the documentation inscribes the existence of an object in history, gives a lifespan to this existence, and gives the object life as such—independently of whether this object was "originally" living or artificial.

The difference between the living and the artificial is, then, exclusively a narrative difference. It cannot be observed but only told, only documented: an object can be given a prehistory, a genesis, an origin by means of narrative. The technical documentation is, incidentally, never constructed as history but always as a system of instructions for producing particular objects under given circumstances. The artistic documentation, whether real or fictive, is, by contrast, primarily narrative, and thus it evokes the unrepeatability of living time. The artificial can thus be made living, made natural, by means of art documentation, by narrating the history of its origin, its "making." Art documentation is thus the art of making living things out of artificial ones, a living activity out of technical practice: it is a bio-art that is simultaneously biopolitics.

This basic function of art documentation was strikingly demonstrated by Ridley Scott's *Blade Runner*. In the film, the artificially produced humans, called "replicants," are given photographic documentation at the time they are produced, which is supposed to certify their "natural origin"—faked photographs of their family, residences, and so on. Although this documentation is fictive, it gives the replicants life—subjectivity—which makes them indistinguishable from the "natural" human beings on the "inside" as well as on the outside. Because the replicants are inscribed in life, in history, by means of this documentation, they can continue this life in an uninterrupted and thoroughly individual way. Consequently, the hero's search for a "real," objectively determinable distinction between the natural and the artificial ultimately proves to be futile, because, as we have seen, this distinction can be established only through an artistically documented narrative.

The fact that life is something that can be documented but not immediately experienced is not a new discovery. One could even claim that this is the definition of life: life can be documented but not shown. In his book

Homo Sacer, Giorgio Agamben points out that the "bare life" has yet to achieve any political and cultural representation.[2] Agamben himself proposes that we view the concentration camp as the cultural representation of the bare life, because its inmates are robbed of all forms of political representation—the only thing that can be said of them is that they are alive. They can therefore only be killed, not sentenced by a court or sacrificed through a religious ritual. Agamben believes that this kind of life outside all laws yet anchored in law is paradigmatic of life itself. Even if there is much to be said for such a definition of life, it must be remembered that life in a concentration camp is generally thought to be beyond our powers of observation or imagination. Life in a concentration camp can be reported—it can be documented—but it cannot be presented for view.[3] Art documentation thus describes the realm of biopolitics by showing how the living can be replaced by the artificial, and how the artificial can be made living by means of a narrative. A few examples will illustrate the different strategies of documentation.

In the late 1970s and early 1980s, the Moscow group Kollektivnye Deystviya (Collective Action Group) organized a series of performances, conceived mostly by the artist Andrey Monastyrsky, which took place outside Moscow with only the members of the group and a few invited guests present. These performances were made accessible to a wider audience only through documentation, in the form of photographs and texts.[4] The texts did not so much describe the performances themselves as the experiences, thoughts, and emotions of those who took part in them—and as a result, they had a strongly narrative, literary character. These highly minimalist performances took place on a white, snow-covered field—a white surface that recalled the white background of Kazimir Malevich's Suprematist paintings, which has become the trademark of the Russian avant-garde. At the same time, however, the significance of this white background, which Malevich had introduced as the symbol of the radical "non-objectivity" of his art, as a symbol of a radical break with all nature and all narrative, was completely transformed. Equating the Suprematist "artificial" white background with the "natural" Russian snow transposed the "non-objective" art of Malevich back into life—specifically, by using a narrative text that attributed another genealogy to (or rather, imposed that genealogy upon) the white of Suprematism. Malevich's paintings thus lose the character of autonomous artworks and are in turn reinterpreted as the documentation of a lived experience—in the snows of Russia.

This reinterpretation of the Russian avant-garde is even more direct in the work of another Moscow artist from this period, Francisco Infante, who in his performance *Posvyashchenie* (Dedication) spread one of Malevich's Suprematist compositions on the snow—once again replacing the white background with snow. A fictive "living" genealogy is attributed to Malevich's painting, as a result of which the painting is led out of art history and into life—as with the replicants in *Blade Runner*. This transformation of the artwork into documentation of a life event opens up a space where all sorts of other genealogies could equally be discovered or invented, several of them quite plausible historically: for example, the white background of the Suprematist paintings can also be interpreted as the white piece of paper that serves as the background for every kind of bureaucratic, technological, or artistic documentation. In this sense, it could also be said that the documentation also has snow as its background—and thus the play of narrative inscriptions can be extended further and further.

Such a drama of narrative inscriptions is also staged in Sophie Calle's installations "Les aveugles" (The Blind) and "Blind Color." "Les aveugles," of 1986, documents a survey the artist conducted in which people who were born blind were asked to describe their conception of beauty. Several responses referred to figurative artworks, about which these blind people had heard, which were said to depict the real, visible world in an especially impressive manner. In her installation, the artist confronts the descriptions of these artworks given by the blind with reproductions of the paintings described. For "Blind Color" of 1991, Calle asked blind people to describe what they see, then wrote their answers on panels, which she juxtaposed with texts on monochrome painting written by artists such as Kazimir Malevich, Yves Klein, Gerhard Richter, Piero Manzoni, and Ad Reinhardt. In these art documentations, which are presented as the results of sociological research, the artist manages to attribute unfamiliar genealogy to the relatively familiar examples of the traditional, figurative, mimetic art, as well as to the examples of modern paintings that are usually understood as artificial, abstract, and autonomous. For the blind the mimetic, figurative paintings become totally fictional, artificially constructed—one can say even autonomous. By contrast, the modernist monochromes show themselves as true depictions of the blind's vision. Here it becomes obvious to what extent our understanding of a particular artwork is dependent on its functioning as document of a certain life situation.

Finally, we should mention here Carsten Höller's performance, *The Baudouin/Boudewijn Experiment: A Large-Scale, Non-Fatalistic Experiment in Deviation,* which took place in the Atomium in Brussels in 2001. A group of people was enclosed in the interior of one of the spheres that make up the Atomium, where they spent an entire day cut off from the outside world. Höller frequently engages in transforming the "abstract," minimalist spaces of radically modernist architecture into spaces for living experience—another way of transforming art into life by means of documentation. In this case, he chose for his performance a space that embodies a utopian dream and does not immediately suggest a domestic environment. Primarily, however, the work alludes to commercial television shows such as *Big Brother,* with its portrayal of people forced to spend a long time together in an enclosed space. But here the difference between a commercial television documentation and art documentation becomes particularly clear. Precisely because television time and again shows images of the enclosed people, the viewer begins to suspect manipulation, constantly asking what might be happening in the space hidden behind these images in which "real" life takes place. By contrast, Höller's performance is not shown but merely documented—specifically, by means of the participants' narratives, which describe precisely that which could not be seen. Here, then, life is understood as something narrated and documented but unable to be shown or presented. This lends the documentation a plausibility of representing life that a direct visual presentation cannot possess.

Topology of the Aura

Some of the examples above are particularly relevant to the analysis of art documentation because they show how famous artworks that are well known in the history of art can be used in a new way—not as art but as documentation. At the same time they also reveal the procedures by which art documentation is produced, along with the difference between the artwork and art documentation. But one important question remains unanswered: if life is only documented by narrative and cannot be shown, then how can such a documentation be shown in an art space without perverting its nature? Art documentation is usually shown in the context of an installation. The installation, however, is an art form in which not only the images, texts, or other elements of which it is composed but also the space itself plays a decisive role. This space is not abstract or neutral but is itself an artwork and at the same time a life space. The placing of documentation in an installation as the act of inscription in a particular space is thus not a neutral act of showing but an act that achieves at the level of space what narrative achieves at the level of time: the inscription in life. The way in which this mechanism functions can best be described by using Walter Benjamin's concept of aura, which he introduced precisely with the intention of distinguishing between the living space of the artwork and its technical substitute, which has no site or context.

Benjamin's essay "The Work of Art in the Age of Mechanical Reproduction" became famous primarily for its use of the concept of aura. Since then, the concept of aura has had a long career in philosophy, especially in the celebrated phrase "loss of aura," which characterizes the fate of the original in the modern age. This emphasis on the loss of aura is, on the one hand, legitimate, and clearly conforms to the overall intention of Benjamin's text. On the other hand, it begs the question of how the aura originates before it can or must be lost. Here, of course, we speak of aura not in the general sense, as a religious or theosophical concept, but in the specific sense used by Benjamin. A close reading of Benjamin's text makes clear that the aura originates only by virtue of the modern technology of reproduction—that is to say, it emerges in the same moment as it is lost. And it emerges for the same reason for which it is lost.

In his essay, Benjamin begins with the possibility of perfect reproduction, in which it is no longer possible to distinguish materially, visually, empirically between the original and the copy. Again and again in his text, Benjamin insists on this perfection. He speaks of technical reproduction as a "most perfect reproduction" which is able to keep intact the material qualities of the actual work of art.[5] Now, it is certainly open to doubt whether the techniques of reproduction that existed at that time, or even today, ever in fact achieved such a degree of perfection that it was impossible to distinguish empirically between the original and the copy. For Benjamin, however, the ideal possibility of such perfect reproducibility, or a perfect cloning, is more important that the technical possibilities that actually existed in his day. The question he raises is: Does the extinction of the material distinction between original and copy mean the extinction of this distinction itself?

Benjamin answers this question in the negative. The disappearance of any material distinction between the original and the copy—or, at least, its potential disappearance—does not eliminate another, invisible but no less real distinction between them: the original has an aura that the copy does not. Thus the notion of aura becomes necessary as a criterion for distinguishing between original and copy only because the technology of reproduction has rendered all material criteria useless. And this means that the concept of aura, and aura itself, belongs exclusively to modernity. Aura is, for Benjamin, the relationship of the artwork to the site in which it is found—the relationship to its external context. The soul of the artwork is not in its body; rather, the body of the artwork is found in its aura, in its soul.

This other topology of the relationship between the soul and the body traditionally has a place in gnosis, in theosophy, and similar schools of thought, which it would not be appropriate to pursue here. The important realization is that for Benjamin the distinction between original and copy is exclusively a topological one—and as such it is entirely independent of the material nature of the work. The original has a particular site—and through this particular site the original is inscribed into history as this unique object. The copy, by contrast, is virtual, siteless, ahistorical: from the beginning it appears as potential multiplicity. To reproduce something is to remove it from its site, to deterritorialize it—reproduction transposes the artwork into the network of topologically undetermined circulation. Benjamin's formulations are well known: "Even the most perfect reproduction of a work of art is lacking in one element: its here and now, its unique existence at the place where it happens to be."[6] He continues: "These 'here' and 'now' of the original constitute the concept of its authenticity, and lay basis for the notion of a tradition that has up to the present day passed this object along as something having a self and an identity."[7] The copy lacks authenticity, therefore, not because it differs from the original but because it has no location and consequently is not inscribed in history.

Thus, for Benjamin, technical reproduction as such is by no means the reason for the loss of aura. The loss of aura is introduced only with a new aesthetic taste—the taste of the modern consumer who prefers the copy or the reproduction to the original. Today's consumer of art prefers art to be brought—delivered. Such a consumer does not want to go off, travel to another place, be placed in another context, in order to experience the original as original. Rather, he or she wants the original to come to him or her—as in fact it does, but only as a copy. When the distinction between original and copy is a topological one, then the topologically defined movement of the viewer alone defines this distinction. If we make our way to the artwork, then it is an original. If we force the artwork to come to us, then it is a copy. For that reason, the distinction between original and copy has, in Benjamin's work, a dimension of violence. In fact, Benjamin speaks not just of the loss of aura but of its destruction.[8] And the violence of this destruction of aura is not lessened by the fact that the aura is invisible. On the contrary, a material injury to the original is much less violent, in Benjamin's view, because it still inscribes itself in the history of the original by leaving behind certain traces on its body. The deterritorialization of the original, its removal from its site by means of bringing it closer represents, by contrast, an invisible and thus all the more devastating employment of violence, because it leaves behind no material trace.

Benjamin's new interpretation of the distinction between original and copy thus opens up the possibility not only of making a copy out of an original but also of making an original out of a copy. Indeed, when the distinction between original and copy is merely a topological, contextual one, then it not only becomes possible to remove an original from its site and deterritorialize it, but also to reterritorialize the copy. Benjamin himself calls attention to this possibility when he writes about the figure of profane illumination and refers to the forms of life that can lead to such a profane illumination: "The reader, the thinker, the loiterer, the *flâneur*, are types of illuminati just as much as the opium eater, the dreamer, the ecstatic."[9] One is struck by the fact that these figures of profane illumination are also figures of motion—especially the *flâneur*. The *flâneur* does not demand of things that they come to him; he goes to things. In this sense, the *flâneur* does not destroy the auras of things; he respects them. Or rather, only through him does the aura emerge again. The figure of profane illumination is the reversal of the "loss of aura" that comes from siting the copy in a topology of undetermined circulation though the modern mass media. Now, however, it is clear that the installation can also be counted among the figures of profane illumination, because it transforms the viewer into a *flâneur*.

Art documentation, which by definition consists of images and texts that are reproducible, acquires through the installation an aura of the original, the living, the historical. In the installation the documentation gains a site—the here and now of a historical event. Because the distinction between original and copy is entirely a topological and situational one, all of the documents placed in the installation become originals. If reproduction makes copies out of originals, installation makes originals out of copies. That means: The fate of modern and contemporary art can by no means be reduced to the "loss of aura." Rather, (post)modernity enacts a complex play of removing from sites and placing in (new) sites, of deterritorialization and reterritorialization, of removing aura and restoring aura. What distinguishes the modern age from earlier periods in this is simply the fact that the originality of a modern work is not determined by its material nature but by its aura, by its context, by its historical site. Consequently, as Benjamin emphasizes, originality does not represent an eternal value. In the modern age, originality has not simply been lost—it has become variable. Otherwise, the eternal value of originality would simply have been replaced by the eternal (non)value of unoriginality—as indeed happens in some art theories. All the same, eternal copies can no more exist than eternal originals. To be an original and possess an aura means the same thing as to be alive. But life is not something that the living being has "in itself." Rather, it is the inscription of a certain being into a life context—into a lifespan and into a living space.

This also reveals the deeper reason why art documentation now serves as a field of biopolitics—and reveals the deeper dimension of modern biopolitics in general. On the one hand, the modern age is constantly substituting the artificial, the technically produced, and the simulated for the real, or (what amounts to the same thing) the reproducible for the unique. It is no coincidence that cloning has become today's emblem of biopolitics, for it is precisely in cloning—no matter whether it ever becomes reality or forever remains a fantasy—that we perceive life as being removed from its site, which is perceived as the real threat of contemporary technology. In reaction to this threat, conservative, defensive strategies are offered which try to prevent this removal of life from its site by means of regulations and bans, even though the futility of such efforts is obvious even to those struggling for them. What is overlooked in this is that the modern age clearly has, on the other hand, strategies for making something living and original from something artificial and reproduced. The practices of art documentation and of installation in particular reveal another path for biopolitics: rather than fighting off modernity, they develop strategies of resisting and of inscription based on situation and context, which make it possible to transform the artificial into something living and the repetitive into something unique.

Iconoclasm as an Artistic Device: Iconoclastic Strategies in Film

Film has never inhabited a sacred context. From its very inception film proceeded through the murky depths of profane and commercial life, always a bedfellow of cheap mass entertainment. Even the attempts to glorify film undertaken by twentieth-century totalitarian regimes never really succeeded—all that resulted was the short-lived enlistment of film for their various propaganda purposes. The reasons for this are not necessarily to be found in the character of film as a medium: film simply arrived too late. By the time film emerged, culture had already shed its potential for consecration. So, given cinema's secular origins it would at first sight seem inappropriate to associate iconoclasm with film. At best, film appears capable only of staging and illustrating historical scenes of iconoclasm, but never of being iconoclastic itself.

What nonetheless can be claimed is that throughout its history as a medium film has waged a more or less open struggle against other media such as painting, sculpture, architecture, and even theater and opera. These can all boast of sacred origins that within present-day culture still afford them their status as aristocratic, "high" arts. Yet the destruction of precisely these high cultural values has been repeatedly depicted and celebrated in film. So, cinematic iconoclasm operates less in relation to a religious or ideological struggle than it does in terms of the conflict between different media; this is an iconoclasm conducted not against its own sacred provenance but against other media. By the same token, in the course of the long history of antagonism between various media, film has earned the right to act as the icon of secular modernity. Inversely, by being transferred into the traditional realm of art, film itself has in turn increasingly become the subject of iconoclastic gestures: by means of new technology such as video, computers, and DVDs, the motion of the film image has been halted midstream and dissected.

In historical terms the iconoclastic gesture has never functioned as an expression of a skeptical attitude toward the truth of the image. Such a skeptical attitude is mirrored more in dispassionate curiosity toward a plethora of religious aberrations, compounded by the well-meaning museum conservation of the historical evidence of such aberrations—and it is certainly not accompanied by the destruction of this evidence. The desecration of ancient idols is performed only in the name of other, more recent gods. Iconoclasm's purpose is to prove that the old gods have lost their power and are subsequently no longer able to defend their earthly temples and images. Thus the iconoclast shows how earnestly he takes the gods' claims to power by contesting the authority of the old gods and asserting the power of his own. In this vein, to cite but a few examples, the temples of pagan religions were destroyed in the name of Christianity, Catholic churches were despoiled in the name of a Protestant interpretation of Christianity, and, later on, all kinds of Christian churches were wrecked in the name of the religion of Reason—which was considered more powerful than the authority of the old biblical god. In turn, the power of reason as manifested by a particular, humanistically defined human image was later iconoclastically attacked in the name of the state-sponsored crusade to maximize productive forces, to secure the omnipotence of technology and to promote the total mobilization of society—at least in central and eastern Europe. And just recently we witnessed the ceremonious dismantling and removal of the fallen idols of Socialism, this time in the name of the even more powerful religion of unrestrained consumerism. It seems that at some point technological progress was realized to be dependent upon consumption, fully in keeping with the adage that supply is generated by demand. So, for the time being, commodity brands will remain our latest household gods, at least until some new, nascent iconoclastic anger rises up against them too.

Iconoclasm can thus be said to function as a mechanism of historical innovation, as a means of revaluing values through a process of constantly destroying old values and introducing new ones in their place. This explains why the iconoclastic gesture always seems to point in the same historical direction, at least as long as history is perceived in the Nietzschean tradition as the history of escalating power. From this perspective iconoclasm appears as a series of progressive, historically ascending movements constantly clearing their path of all that has become redundant, powerless, and void of inner meaning, to make way for whatever the future might bring. This is why all criticism of iconoclasm has traditionally had a reactionary aftertaste.

However, such a close connection between iconoclasm and historical progress is not logically necessary, for iconoclasm addresses not only the old but also the new: in the early stages of their mission, devotees of new gods have always been subjected to persecution and the desecration of their symbols, be they the first Christians, revolutionaries, Marxists, or even hippies, those martyrs of consumerism and fashion. Essentially, on each occasion this persecution is also a signal that the new gods are not powerful enough, or at least not as powerful as the old gods. And in many cases, this gesture has proved altogether effective: the new religious movements were suppressed and the power of the old gods reasserted. Of course one can, if one so wishes, put a Hegelian spin on this and see it as evidence of the ruse of reason lending reactionary support to the march of progress. Characteristically, however, rather than such gestures of suppression and destruction leveled at new movements being viewed as iconoclastic, they are generally seen as the martyrization of what is new. Indeed, most religions foster iconographic canons composed of images that depict their earlier martyrdom. In this respect, it can be said that each religion's iconography preempts any iconoclastic gesture that this religion might fall victim to. The sole factor distinguishing this anticipated from actual destruction is that survival (in the first case) rather than downfall (in the second case) is upheld as the object of aspiration and celebration. This difference can be equated with the contrasting positions of victor and vanquished—whereby the observer is free to choose which of the two sides he prefers to identify with, all depending on his personal view of history.

History is also made up more of revivals than of innovations, whereby most innovations make their appearance as revivals and most revivals as innovations. On closer inspection, one gradually loses all hope of determining which historical force ultimately ends up the victor in order to distinguish between iconoclasm and martyrdom. For here there can be no question of "ultimately": history presents itself as a sequence of revaluations of values without any discernible overarching direction. Moreover, we really have no way of knowing whether a defeat means a decline, or a victory an increase in power. Defeat and martyrdom both contain a promise that is lacking in victory. Victory leads to its "appropriation" by the status quo, whereas defeat might possibly turn into a later, ultimate victory capable of revaluing the status quo. Indeed, since at least the death of Christ, the iconoclastic gesture has proved a failure, essentially because it instantly reveals itself as celebration of its purported victim. In light of the Christian tradition, the image of destruction left behind by the iconoclastic gesture is quasi-automatically transformed into the victim's image of triumph, long before the later resurrection or historical revaluation "really" takes place. Conditioned by Christianity over considerable time, our iconographic imagination now no longer needs to wait before acknowledging victory in defeat: here, defeat is equated with victory from the outset.

How this mechanism functions in the post-Christian modern world can be clearly demonstrated with the example of the historical avant-garde. It can be said that the avant-garde is nothing other than a staged martyrdom of the image that replaced the Christian image of martyrdom. After all, the avant-garde abuses the body of the traditional image with all manner of torture utterly reminiscent of the torture inflicted on the body of Christ in the iconography of medieval Christianity.[1] In its treatment by the avant-garde, the image is—in both symbolic and literal terms—sawed apart, cut up, smashed into fragments, pierced, spiked, drawn through dirt, and exposed to ridicule. It is also no accident that the vocabulary used by the historical avant-garde in its manifestos reproduces the language of iconoclasm. We find mentions of discarding traditions, breaking with conventions, destroying old art, and eradicating outdated values. This is by no means driven by some sadistic urge to cruelly maltreat the bodies of innocent images. Nor is all this wreckage and destruction intended to clear the way for the emergence of new images and the introduction of new values. Far from it, for it is the images of wreckage and destruction themselves that serve as the icons of new values. In the eyes of the avant-garde the iconoclastic gesture represents an artistic device, deployed less as a means of destroying old icons than as a way to generate new images—or, indeed, new icons.

However, this possibility of strategically deploying iconoclasm as an artistic device came about because the avant-garde for its part shifted its focus from the message to the medium. The destruction of old images embodying a particular message is not meant to generate new images embodying a new message but rather to highlight the materiality of the medium concealed behind any "spiritual" message. The stuff that art is made of can only be made visible once the image ceases to serve as the manifestation of a specific "conscious" artistic message. Hence, in the artistic practice of the avant-garde the iconoclastic gesture is arguably also intended as a means of removing what has grown old and powerless and asserting the supremacy of the powerful.

Yet this is no longer practiced in pursuit of a new religious or ideological message but in the name of the power of the medium itself. It is significant that Malevich, for example, speaks of the "Suprematism of painting" that he hopes to achieve with his art—by which he means painting in its pure, material form, in its superiority over the spirit.[2] With this, the avant-garde can be said to have celebrated the victory of the powerful—*qua* material—artistic media over the powerless, null medium "spirit," to which these media had hitherto been subordinated for far too long. Accordingly, the process of destroying old icons is rendered identical to the process of generating new ones—in this case, the icons of materialism. The image is thereby transfigured into the site for an epiphany of pure matter, abandoning its role as the site for an epiphany of the spirit.

However, this transition from the spiritual to the material within traditional arts like painting and sculpture ultimately remained beyond the comprehension of the wider audience—neither medium was considered powerful enough. The real turning point came with film. In this context Walter Benjamin has already pointed out that the practices of fragmentation and collage—in other words, the unmitigated martyrdom of the image—were swiftly accepted when they were displayed in film, but greeted by the same audience with outrage and rejection in the context of the traditional arts. Benjamin's explanation for this phenomenon is that as a new medium film is culturally unencumbered: The change of medium thereby justifies the introduction of new artistic strategies.[3]

Furthermore, film also appears to be more powerful than the old media. The reason for this lies not merely in its reproducibility and the system for its mass commercial distribution: Film also seems to be of equal rank to the spirit because it too moves in time. Accordingly, film operates analogously to the way consciousness works, therein proving capable of substituting for the movement of consciousness. As Gilles Deleuze correctly observes, film transforms its viewers into spiritual automata: Film unfurls inside the viewer's head in lieu of his own stream of consciousness.[4] Yet this reveals film's fundamental character to be deeply ambivalent. On the one hand, film is a celebration of movement, the proof of its superiority over all other media; on the other, however, it places its audience in a state of unparalleled physical and mental immobility. It is this ambivalence that dictates a variety of filmic strategies, including iconoclastic strategies.

Indeed, as a medium of motion, film is frequently eager to display its superiority over other media, whose greatest accomplishments are preserved in the form of immobile cultural treasures and monuments, by staging and celebrating the destruction of these monuments. At the same time, this tendency also demonstrates film's adherence to the typically modern faith in the superiority of the *vita activa* over the *vita contemplativa*. Every kind of iconophilia is ultimately rooted in a fundamentally contemplative approach and in a general readiness to treat certain objects deemed sacred exclusively as objects of distant, admiring contemplation. This disposition is based on the taboo that protects these objects from being touched, from being intimately penetrated and, more generally, from the profanity of being integrated into the practices of daily life. In film nothing is deemed so holy that it might or ought to be safeguarded from being absorbed into the general flow of movement. Everything film shows is translated into movement and thereby profaned. In this respect, film manifests its complicity with the philosophies of *praxis*, of *Lebensdrang*, of the *élan vital* and of desire; it parades its collusion with ideas that, in the footsteps of Marx and Nietzsche, captured the imagination of European humanity at the end of the nineteenth and the beginning of the twentieth centuries—in other words, during the very period that gave birth to film as a medium. This was the era when the hitherto prevailing attitude of passive contemplation, which was capable of shaping ideas rather than reality, was displaced by adulation of the potent movements of material forces. In this act of worship film plays a central role. From its very inception film has celebrated everything that moves at high speed—trains, cars, airplanes—but also everything that goes beneath the surface—blades, bombs, bullets.

Likewise, from the moment it emerged film has used slapstick comedy to stage veritable orgies of destruction, demolishing anything that just stands or hangs motionlessly, including traditionally revered cultural treasures, and sparing not even public spectacles such as theater and opera that embodied the spirit of old culture. Designed to provoke all-round laughter in the audience, these movie scenes of destruction, wreckage, and demolition are reminiscent of Bakhtin's theory of carnival that both emphasizes and affirms the cruel, destructive aspects of carnival.[5] Of all preceding art forms, it is no surprise that the circus and the carnival were treated with such positive deference by film in its early days. Bakhtin described the carnival as an iconoclastic celebration that exuded an aura of joy rather than serious, emotional, or revolutionary sentiment; instead of causing the violated icons of the old order to be supplanted by the icons of some new order, the carnival invited us to revel in the downfall of the status quo. Bakhtin also writes about how the general carnivalization of European culture in the modern era compensates for the decline of "real" social practices traditionally provided by the carnival. Although Bakhtin draws his examples from literature, his descriptions of carnivalized art apply equally well to the strategies with which some of the most famous images in film history were produced.

At the same time Bakhtin's carnival theory also emphasizes just how inherently contradictory iconoclastic carnivalism is in film. Historical carnivals were participatory, offering the entire population the chance to take part in a festive form of collective iconoclasm. But once iconoclasm is used strategically as an artistic device, the community is automatically excluded—and becomes an audience. Indeed, while film as such is a celebration of movement, it paradoxically drives the audience to new extremes of immobility never reached by traditional art forms. It is possible to move around with relative freedom while one is reading or viewing an exhibition, but in the movie theater the viewer is cast in darkness and glued to his or her seat. The situation of the moviegoer in fact resembles a grandiose parody of the very *vita contemplativa* that film itself denounces, because the cinema system embodies precisely that *vita contemplativa* as it surely appears from the perspective of its most radical critic—an uncompromising Nietzschean, let us say—namely as the product of a vitiated lust for life and dwindling personal initiative, as a token of compensatory consolation and a sign of individual inadequacy in real life. This is the starting point of any critique of film which is building up to a new iconoclastic gesture—an iconoclasm due to be turned against film itself. Criticism of audience passivity first led to various attempts to use film as a means of activating a mass audience, of politically mobilizing or injecting movement into it. Sergei Eisenstein, for instance, was exemplary in the way he combined aesthetic shock with political propaganda in an endeavor to rouse the viewer and wrench him from his passive, contemplative condition.

But as time passed, it became clear that it was precisely the illusion of movement generated by film that drove the viewer toward passivity. This insight is nowhere better formulated than in Guy Debord's *The Society of the*

Spectacle, a book whose themes and rhetorical figures continue to resound throughout the current debate on mass culture. Not without reason, he describes present-day society, defined as it is by the electronic media, as a total cinema event. For Debord, the entire world has become a movie theater in which people are completely isolated from one another and from real life, and are consequently condemned to an existence of utter passivity.[6] As he vividly demonstrates in his final film *In girim imus nocte et consumimur igni* (1978), this condition can no longer be remedied with increased velocity, intensified mobility, the escalation of emotions, aesthetic shock, or further political propaganda. What is required instead is the abolition of the illusion of movement generated by film; only then will viewers gain the chance to rediscover their ability to move. In the name of real social movement, filmic motion has to be stopped and brought to a standstill.

This marks the beginning of an iconoclastic movement against film, and consequently of the martyrdom of film. This iconoclastic protest has the same root cause as all other iconoclastic movements; it represents a revolt against a passive, contemplative mode of conduct waged in the name of movement and activity. But where film is concerned, the outcome of this protest might at first sight seem somewhat paradoxical. Since film images are actually moving images, the immediate result of the iconoclastic gesture performed against film is petrifaction and an interruption of the film's natural dynamism. The instruments of film's martyrdom are various new technologies such as video, computers, and DVDs. These new digital technologies make it possible to arrest a film's flow at any moment whatsoever, providing evidence that a film's motion is neither real nor material, but simply an illusion that can equally well be digitally simulated. In the following, I discuss both iconoclastic gestures—the destruction of prevailing religious and cultural icons through film, and the exposure of film's movement itself as an illusion.

Let us illustrate these various filmic strategies by selected examples which cannot, of course, claim to cover all aspects of iconoclastic practices, but nonetheless offer insight into their logic.

The image of the lacerated eye in *Un chien andalou* (1929) by Luis Buñuel is one of the most famous film icons of its kind. The scene heralds not only the destruction of a particular image, but also the suppression of the contemplative attitude itself. The meditative, theoretical gaze, intent on observing the world as a whole and thereby reflecting itself as a purely spiritual, disembodied entity, is referred back to its material, physiological state. This transforms the very act of seeing into an altogether material and, if one so wishes, blind activity, a process that Merleau-Ponty, for instance, later formulated as palpating the world with the eye.[7] This could be described as a meta-iconoclastic gesture, one that renders it sheerly impossible to pursue visual adoration from a religious or aesthetic distance. The film shows the eye as pure matter—and hence vulnerable to being touched, if not destroyed. As a demonstration of how physical, material force has the power to eradicate contemplation, this image of movement acts as an epiphany of the world's pure materiality.

This blind, purely material, destructive force is embodied—if somewhat more naively—by the figure of Samson in Cecil B. DeMille's 1949 movie *Samson and Delilah*. In the film's central scene, Samson destroys a heathen temple along with all the idols assembled there—thus bringing on the symbolic collapse of the entire old order. But Samson is not depicted as the bearer of a new religion, or of enlightenment; he is simply a blind titan, a body wielding the same blind destruction as an earthquake. Acting with a convulsiveness on a par with this is the revolutionary, iconoclastic crowd we encounter in Sergei Eisenstein's films. In the realm of social and political action, these human masses represent the blind, material forces that covertly govern consciously perceived human history—exactly as the Marxist philosophy of history describes them. Historically, these masses move to destroy those monuments designed to immortalize the individual (in Eisenstein's *October* it is the monument to the tsar). But the widespread exhilaration with which this anonymous work of destruction is greeted as a revelation of the material "madeness" of culture is also accompanied by the sadistic, voyeuristic pleasure felt by Eisenstein on watching such iconoclastic acts, as he readily admits in his memoirs.[8]

This erotic, sadistic component of iconoclasm can be sensed even more forcefully in the famous scene in which the "False Maria" is burnt in Fritz Lang's *Metropolis* (1926). But the blind anger of the masses that erupts here is not revolutionary but counterrevolutionary: although the revolutionary agitator is burnt like a witch, she is clearly modeled on the symbolic female figures that since the French Revolution have embodied the ideals of freedom, the republic, and revolution. However, as she is burning, this beautiful, enchanting female figure capable of "luring" the masses is exposed as a robot. The flames destroy the female idol of the revolution, unmasking her as a mechanical, nonhuman construct. The whole scene has a thoroughly barbaric ring about it, particularly at the beginning when we are still unaware that "False Maria" is a machine insensitive to pain and not a living human being. The demise of this revolutionary idol also paves the way for the true Maria whose arrival restores social harmony by reconciling father and son, the upper and lower classes. So, rather than serving the new religion of social revolution, iconoclasm here acts in the interests of the restoration of traditional Christian values. Yet the cinematic means Lang draws upon to depict the iconoclastic masses are not dissimilar from those employed by Eisenstein: In both cases the crowd operates as an elementary material force.

There is a direct link between these early films and countless, more recent movies in which the Earth itself, currently acting as the icon of the latest religion of globalization, is destroyed by forces from outer space. In *Armageddon* (1998, dir. Michael Bay) these come in the form of purely material, cosmic forces that act according to the laws of nature and remain utterly indifferent to the significance of our planet, along with all the civilizations it quarters. The destruction of icons of civilization such as Paris primarily illustrates the transience of all human civilizations and their iconographies. The aliens featured in *Independence Day* (1996, dir. Roland Emmerich) might be portrayed as intelligent and civilized beings, but their actions are driven by an inner compulsion to annihilate all creatures of different origin. In the movie's key scene where New York is wiped out, the viewer can easily spot Emmerich's indirect polemic against the famous scenes in Steven Spielberg's *Close Encounters of the Third Kind* depicting the arrival of the aliens. Whereas Spielberg automatically associates the aliens' high intelligence with a peace-loving nature, the superior intelligence of the aliens in *Independence Day* is allied to an unbounded appetite for total evil. Here, the Other is portrayed not as a partner but as a lethal threat.

This inversion is pursued with even greater clarity and consistency by Tim Burton. In *Mars Attacks!* (1996) the chief Martian unleashes his campaign of destruction with the thoroughly iconoclastic gesture of shooting the peace dove that was released as a token of welcome by the gullible and humanistically indoctrinated Earthlings. To humankind this iconoclastic gesture heralds its physical annihilation rather than a new wave of enlightenment. Not restricted to violence against doves, the same threat is also signaled by violence against images. As the antihero of Burton's *Batman* (1989), the Joker is presented as an avant-garde, iconoclastic artist bent on destroying the classical paintings in a museum by overpainting them in a kind of abstract expressionist style. Furthermore, the entire overpainting sequence is shot in the manner of a cheerful music video clip, a *mise-en-scène* of artistic iconoclasm that bears great affinity to Bakhtin's description of the carnivalesque. But rather than lending the iconoclastic gesture cultural significance and neutralizing it by inscribing it into the carnival tradition, the carnivalesque mood of this scene only emphasizes and radicalizes its iniquity.

Tracey Moffatt's short film *Artist* (1999) quotes various more or less well-known feature films that all tell the story of an artist. Each of these stories opens with an artist hoping to create a masterpiece; this is followed by him proudly presenting the accomplished work of art and closes with the work being destroyed personally by the disappointed, despairing artist. At the end of this film collage Moffatt stages a veritable orgy of artistic destruction using appropriate footage. Pictures and sculptures of various styles are shredded, burnt, smashed, and blown up. The film collage thereby offers a precise résumé of the treatment cinema has meted out to traditional art forms. But let it not go unmentioned that the artist also subjects film itself to a process of deconstruction. She fragments individual movies, interrupts their movement and corrupts their subjects beyond recognition, mixing up the fragments of these various, stylistically disparate films to create a new, monstrous filmic body. The resultant film collage is clearly not intended for screening in a movie theater but for presentation in traditional art spaces such as galleries or museums. Tracey Moffatt's film not only reflects on the abuse inflicted on art in film, but in a subtle manner also exacts revenge for its suffering.

In other more recent movies, such scenes of iconoclasm are by no means an occasion for celebration. Present-day cinema is not revolutionary, even if it still feeds off the tradition of revolutionary iconoclasm. For, as ever, film never ceases to articulate the unattainability of peace, stability or calm in a world agog with movement and violence—and, by the same token, the absence of material conditions that would afford us a secure, contemplative and iconophilic existence. As ever, the status quo is routinely brought crashing down and irony is poured on the trust held by traditional art forms in the power of their motionless images—after all, even the symbol of the peace dove was modeled on an equally famous picture by Picasso. The difference now is that iconoclasm is no longer considered to be an expression of humanity's hopes of liberation from the power of the old idols. Since the currently dominant humanistic iconography has placed humanity itself in the foreground, the iconoclastic gesture is now inevitably seen as the expression of radical, inhumane evil, the work of pernicious aliens, vampires, and deranged humanoid machines. Nonetheless, this inversion of iconoclasm's direction is not dictated solely by the current shift in ideology, but is also influenced by immanent developments within film as a medium. The iconoclastic gesture is now increasingly ascribed to the realm of entertainment. Disaster epics, movies about aliens and the end of the world, and vampire thrillers are generally perceived as potential box-office hits—precisely because they most radically celebrate the cinematic illusion of movement. This has spawned a deep-rooted, immanent criticism of film from within the commercial film industry itself, a critical attitude that aspires to bring filmic movement to a standstill.

As an expression and preliminary climax of this intrinsic criticism, we need only turn to *Matrix* (1999, dir. Andy and Larry Wachovski), a movie that, in spite of its furious pace and proliferation of scenes shot at extreme speed, nonetheless stages the end of all movement—including filmic movement. As the film closes, the hero, Neo, gains the ability to perceive all visible reality as a single digitalized film; through the world's visual surface he sees the incessantly moving code flooding down like rain. In what amounts to a deconstructive exposure of filmic movement, the viewer is shown that this is not movement generated by life or by matter, and not even movement of the spirit, but simply the lifeless movement of a digital code. Here, compared with the earlier revolutionary films of the 1920s and 1930s, we are dealing with a different suspicion and, correspondingly, with a differently poised iconoclastic gesture.[9] As a neo-Buddhist, neo-gnostic hero who appears on the scene to take up the fight against the evil creators and *malins génies* ruling the world, Neo is no longer rebelling against the spirit in the name of the material world, but is an agitator rising up against the illusion of the material world in the name of the critique of simulation. Toward the end of the film, Neo is greeted with the words "He is the One." Neo's way of proving his calling as the new, gnostic Christ is precisely to halt the cinematic movement, thereby causing the bullets that are about to strike him to stop in midair.

Here the time-honored, widespread criticism of the movie industry appears to have been adopted by Hollywood as its own theme—and thereby radicalized. As we well know, critics have accused the movie industry of creating a seductive illusion and staging a beautiful semblance of the world designed to mask, conceal, and deny its ugly reality. Then *Matrix* turns up and basically says the same. Except that in this case it is less a cinematographically concocted "beautiful facade" that is paraded before us as a complete *mise-en-scène*, than the whole, everyday, "real" world. In movies like *The Truman Show* or, far more comprehensively, *Matrix*, this so-called reality is presented as if it were a long-running "reality show" produced using quasi-cinematographic techniques in some otherworldly studio hidden beneath the surface of the real world. The main protagonists of such films are heroes of enlightenment, media critics, and private detectives all rolled into one, whose ambition is to expose not only the culture they live in, but indeed also their entire everyday world as an artificially generated illusion.

Of course, in spite of its metaphysical qualities, *Matrix* too is ultimately trapped in the arena of mass entertainment, and Christian values certainly offer no way out of this context—an insight that is ironically and convincingly illustrated in *Monty Python's Life of Brian* (1979). Not only does this film parody and profane the life of Christ, but it also depicts Christ's death on the cross in the carnivalesque fashion of a music video. This scene represents an elegant iconoclastic gesture that channels the martyrdom of Christ into the realm of entertainment (as well as being highly entertaining in its own right). But in the present day, more earnest forms of iconoclasm directed against film are undertaken when film is transferred into the sober context of high art—in other words, into the very context that earlier, revolutionary cinema desired to lay open to cheerful, carnivalesque destruction.

In our culture we have two fundamentally different models at our disposal that give us control over the length of time we spend looking at an image: the immobilization of the image in the exhibition space or the immobilization of the viewer in the movie theater. Yet both models founder when moving images are transferred into the museum or art exhibition space. The images will continue to move—but the viewer does too. Over the past decades video art has made various attempts to resolve the antagonism between these two forms of movement. Today, as in the past, one widespread strategy has been to make the individual video or film sequences as short as possible so as to ensure that the time a viewer spends in front of a work does not substantially exceed the time a viewer might on average be expected to spend in front of a "good" picture in a museum. While there is nothing objectionable about this strategy, it nonetheless represents a missed opportunity to explicitly address the uncertainty caused in the viewer by transferring moving images into the art space. This issue is dealt with most arrestingly by films in which a certain image changes only very minimally—if at all—and in this sense coincides with the traditional presentation in a museum of a solitary, immobile image.

One pioneering example of such "motionless" films (and one that certainly has an iconoclastic effect given how it brings the film image to a standstill) is Andy Warhol's *Empire State Building* (1964)—which is hardly surprising considering that the film's author was highly active in the art world. The film consists of a fixed image that barely changes for hours on end. Unlike the moviegoer, however, an art space visitor would see this film as part of a cinematic installation, sparing him the risk of getting bored. Since the exhibition visitor is not only allowed, but also, as already mentioned, supposed to freely move around the exhibition space, he can leave the room at any time and return to it later. Thus, in contrast to a cinema audience, the visitor to Warhol's exhibited film will not be able to say definitively by the end whether the film consists of a moving or a motionless image, since he will always have to admit the possibility that he might have missed certain events in the film. But it is precisely this uncertainty that explicitly thematizes the relationship between mobile and immobile images within an exhibition context. Time ceases to be experienced as the time taken by the movement shown in a film's image and is instead perceived as the indefinable, problematic duration of the filmic image itself.[10]

The same can be said of Derek Jarman's celebrated film *Blue* (1993), as it can also of *Feature Film* (1999) by Douglas Gordon, a movie that from the outset was conceived as a film installation. In Gordon's work, Hitchcock's masterpiece *Vertigo* is replaced in its entirety by a film presenting nothing but the music to *Vertigo* and, whenever the music is played, images of the conductor conducting this music. For the rest of the time the screen remains black: here the movement of the music has replaced the movement of the film image.

Accordingly, this music acts like a code whose movement is followed by the film, even if on its surface it creates the illusion of "real" movement experienced in the world. This represents the point where the iconoclastic gesture has come full circle: whereas at the beginning of film history it was immobile contemplation that came under attack, by the end the film itself loses its movement, turning into a black rectangle. As one tentatively feels one's way around the blacked-out installation space trying to get a better sense of orientation, it is difficult not to be reminded of the image of the lacerated eye in Buñuel's film—a gesture that already promised to cast the world in darkness.

From Image to Image File—and Back: Art in the Age of Digitalization

The digitalization of the image was initially thought of as a way to escape the museum or, generally, any exhibition space—to set the image free. But in recent decades we have seen the growing presence of digital images in the context of traditional art institutions. So the question arises: What does this fact tell us about digitalization and about these institutions?

On both sides of the digital divide one feels a certain discontent. On one side, the liberated digital image seems to be subjected to a new imprisonment, a new confinement inside the museum and exhibition walls. On the other side, the art system seems to be compromised by exhibiting digital copies instead of originals. Of course, one can argue that the digital photographs or videos—like readymades or analog films and photographs before them—being displayed in the exhibition space demonstrates the loss of aura, the postmodern skepticism toward the modernist notion of originality. But one can doubt that such a demonstration is a sufficient reason for producing and exhibiting the huge amount of digital images that confront us in today's museums and exhibition spaces. And: Why should we exhibit these images at all—instead of just letting them circulate freely in the contemporary information network?

Digitalization would seem to allow the image to become independent of any kind of exhibition practice. Digital images have, that is, an ability to originate, to multiply, and to distribute themselves through the open fields of contemporary means of communication, such as the Internet or cell-phone networks, immediately and anonymously, without any curatorial control. In this respect we can speak of the digital images as genuinely strong images—as images that are able to show themselves according to their own nature, depending solely on their own vitality and strength. Of course, one can always assume that there is a certain hidden curatorial practice and a certain hidden agenda concealed behind any concrete strong image—but such an assumption remains a suspicion that cannot be proven "objectively." So one can say: The digital image is a truly strong image—in the sense that it is not in need of any additional curatorial help to be exhibited, to be seen. But the question arises: Is the digital image also a strong image in the sense that it can stabilize its identity through all its appearances? A strong image can be regarded as truly strong only if it can guarantee its own identity in time—otherwise we are dealing again with a weak image that is dependent on a specific space, the specific context of its presentation.

Now, one can argue that it is not so much the digital image itself as the image file that can be called strong, because the image file remains more or less identical through the process of its distribution. But the image file is not an image—the image file is invisible. Only the heroes of the movie *Matrix* could see the image files, the digital code as such. The relationship between the image file and the image that emerges as an effect of the visualization of this image file—as an effect of its decoding by a computer—can be interpreted as a relationship between original and copy. The digital image is a visible copy of the invisible image file, of the invisible data. In this respect the digital image is functioning as a Byzantine icon—as a visible copy of invisible God. Digitalization creates the illusion that there is no longer any difference between original and copy, and that all we have are the copies that multiply and circulate in the information networks. But there can be no copies without an original. The difference between original and copy is obliterated in the case of digitalization only by the fact that the original data are invisible: they exist in the invisible space behind the image, inside the computer.

So the question arises: How can we possibly grasp this specific condition of the digital image, the data, inside this image itself? The average spectator has no magic pill that would allow him or her like the heroes of *Matrix* to enter the space of the invisibility behind the digital image—to be confronted directly with the digital data itself. And such a spectator has no technique that would allow him or her to transfer the data directly into the brain and to experience it in the mode of pure, nonvisualizable suffering as is done in another movie—*Johnny Mnemonic*. (Actually, pure suffering is, as we know, the most adequate experience of the Invisible.) In this respect, how iconoclastic religions have dealt with the image could probably help. According to these religions the Invisible shows itself in the world not through any specific individual image but through the whole history of its appearances and interventions. Such a history is necessarily ambiguous: It documents the individual appearances or interventions of the Invisible (biblically speaking: signs and wonders) within the topography of the visible world—but at the same time it documents them in a way that relativizes all these appearances and interventions, that avoids the trap of recognizing one specific image as *the* image of the Invisible. The Invisible remains invisible precisely by the multiplication of its visualizations.

Similarly, looking at digital images we are also confronted every time with a new event of visualization of invisible data. So we can say: The digital image is a copy—but the event of its visualization is an original event, because the digital copy is a copy that has no visible original. That further means: A digital image, to be seen, should not be merely exhibited but staged, performed. Here the image begins to function analogously to a piece of music, whose score, as is generally known, is not identical to the musical piece—the score itself being silent. For music to resound, it has to be performed. Thus one can say that digitalization turns the visual arts into a performing art. But to perform something is to interpret it, to betray it, to distort it. Every performance is an interpretation and every interpretation is a betrayal, a misuse. The situation is especially difficult in the case of the invisible original: If the original is visible it can be compared to a copy—so the copy can be corrected and the feeling of betrayal reduced. But if the original is invisible no such comparison is possible—any visualization remains uncertain. Here the figure of the curator arises again—and it becomes even more powerful than it was before, because the curator becomes now not only the exhibitor but the performer of the image. The curator does not simply show an image that was originally there but not seen. Rather, the contemporary curator turns the invisible into the visible.

By doing so the curator makes choices that modify the performed image in a substantial way. The curator does this first of all by selecting the technology that should be used to visualize the image data. The information technology is constantly changing nowadays—hardware, software—simply everything is in flux. Because of this the image is already transformed with every act of visualization using a different, new technology. Today's technology thinks in terms of generations—we speak of computer generations, of generations of photographic and video equipment. But where there are generations, there are also generation conflicts, Oedipal struggles. Anyone who attempts to transfer his or her old text files or image files using a new software will experience the power of the Oedipus complex over current technology—much data gets destroyed, lost in darkness. The biological metaphor says it all: Not only life, which is notorious in this respect, but also technology, which supposedly opposes nature, has become the medium of non-identical reproduction. But even if the technology could guarantee the visual identity of the different visualizations of the same data they would remain non-identical because of the changing context of their appearances.

In his famous essay "The Work of Art in the Age of Mechanical Reproduction" Walter Benjamin assumes the possibility of a technically perfect identical reproduction that no longer allows a material distinction between original and copy. Nevertheless at the same time, a distinction between original and copy remains valid. According to Benjamin, the traditional artwork loses its aura when it is transported from its original place to an exhibition space or when it is copied. But that means that the loss of aura is especially significant in the case of the visualization of an image file. If a traditional "analog" original is moved from one place to another it remains a part of the same space, the same topography—the same visible world. By contrast, the digital original—the file of digital data—is moved by its visualization from the space of invisibility, from the status of "non-image" to the space of visibility, to the status of "image." Accordingly, we have here a truly massive loss of aura—because nothing has more aura than the Invisible. The visualization of the Invisible is the most radical form of its profanation. The visualization of digital data is a sacrilege—comparable to the attempt to visualize or depict the invisible God of Judaism or Islam. And this act of radical profanation cannot be compensated by a set of rules that would enforce the iterability of the visual on the results of this profanation as, for example, happened in the case of the Byzantine icons. As has already been said, modern technology is not capable of establishing such homogeneity.

Benjamin's assumption that an advanced technology can guarantee the material identity between original and copy has not been validated by further technological developments. The actual development of technology went in the opposite direction—in the direction of the diversification of the conditions under which a copy is produced and distributed and, accordingly, the diversification of the resulting visual images. The central characteristic of the Internet consists precisely in the fact that on the Net, all symbols, words, and images are assigned an address: They are placed somewhere, territorialized, inscribed into a certain topology. This means that even beyond the permanent generational differences and corresponding shifts, the fate of digital data on the Internet is essentially dependent on the quality of the specific hardware, server, software, browser, and so on. The individual files may be distorted, interpreted differently, or even rendered unreadable. They may also be attacked by computer viruses, accidentally deleted, or may simply age and perish. In this way, files on the Internet become the heroes of their own story, which, like any story, is primarily one of possible or real loss. Indeed, such stories are told constantly: How certain files can no longer be read, how certain Web sites disappeared, and so on.

The social space in which digitalized images—photographs, videos—are circulating today is also an extremely heterogeneous space. One can visualize videos with the aid of a video recorder, but also as a projection on a screen, on television, within the context of a video installation, on the monitor of a computer, on a cell phone, and so on. In all of these cases, the same video file looks different even on the surface—not to mention the very different social contexts within which it is shown. Digitalization, that is, the writing of the image, helps the image become reproducible, to circulate freely, to distribute itself. It is therefore the medicine that cures the image of its inherent passivity. But at the same time, the digitalized image becomes even more infected with non-identity—with the necessity of presenting the image as dissimilar to itself, which means that supplementary curing of the image—its curating—becomes unavoidable.

Or to put it in another way: It becomes unavoidable to bring the digital image back into the museum, back into the exhibition space. And here, each presentation of a digitalized image becomes a re-creation of this image. Only the traditional exhibition space opens up the possibility for us to reflect not only on the software but also on the hardware, on the material side of the image data. To speak in traditional Marxist terms: The positioning of the digital in the exhibition space makes it possible for the viewer to reflect not only on the superstructure but also on the material basis of digitalization.

This is especially relevant for video, because the video has meanwhile become the leading vehicle of visual communication. When video images are placed in the art exhibition space, they immediately subvert the expectations we generally associate with this space. In the traditional art space, the viewer—at least in the ideal case—has complete control over the duration of his or her contemplation: He or she can interrupt contemplation of a particular image at any time to come back to it later and resume viewing it at the same point it was previously interrupted. While the viewer is absent, the unmoving image remains identical to itself. The production of identity of the image over time constitutes what we refer to in our culture as "high art." In our usual, "normal" lives, the time dedicated to contemplation is clearly dictated by life itself. With respect to real-life images, we do not possess sovereignty, administrative power over the time of contemplation: In life, we are always only accidental witnesses of certain events and certain images, whose duration we cannot control. All art therefore begins with the wish to hold on to a moment, to let it linger for an indeterminate time. Thus the museum—and generally any art exhibition space in which as a rule unmoving images are exhibited—obtains its real justification: It guarantees the ability of the visitor to administer the duration of his attention. However, the situation changes drastically with the introduction of moving images into the museum, as these begin to dictate the time the visitor needs in order to view them—and to rob him of his traditional sovereignty.

In our culture, we have two different models that allow us to gain control over time: The immobilization of the image in the museum, and the immobilization of the audience in the movie theater. Both models, however, fail when moving images are transferred into the space of a museum. In this case, the images go on moving—but the audience also continues to move. One does not remain sitting or standing for any length of time in an exhibition space; rather one retraces one's steps through the space again and again, remains standing in front of a picture for a while, moves closer or away from it, looks at it from different perspectives, and so on. The viewer's movement in the exhibition space cannot be arbitrarily stopped because it is constitutive of the functioning of perception within the art system. In addition, an attempt to force a visitor to watch all of the videos or films in the context of a larger exhibition from beginning to end would be doomed to failure from the start—the duration of the average exhibition visit is simply not long enough.

It is obvious that this causes a situation in which the expectations of a visit to a movie theater and a visit to a museum conflict with each other.

The visitor to a video installation basically no longer knows what to do: Should he stop and watch the images moving before his eyes as in a movie theater, or, as in a museum, continue on in the confidence that over time, the moving images will not change as much as seems likely? Both solutions are clearly unsatisfactory—actually, they are not real solutions at all. One is quickly forced to recognize, though, that there cannot be any adequate or satisfactory solution in this unprecedented situation. Each individual decision to stop or to continue on remains an uneasy compromise—and later has to be revised time and again.

It is precisely this fundamental uncertainty that results when the movement of the images and the movement of the viewer occur simultaneously that creates the added aesthetic value of bringing the digitalized moving images into the exhibition space. In the case of a video installation, a struggle arises between the viewer and the artist over the control of the duration of contemplation. Consequently, the duration of actual contemplation has to be continually renegotiated. Thus the aesthetic value of a video installation consists primarily in explicitly thematicizing the potential invisibility of the image, the viewer's lack of control over the duration of his attention paid in the exhibition space, in which previously the illusion of complete visibility prevailed. The viewer's inability to take complete visual control is further aggravated by the increased speed at which moving images are currently able to be produced.

For the viewer, formerly the investment in terms of work, time, and energy required for consuming a traditional work of art stood in an extremely favorable relation to the duration of art production. After the artist had to spend a long time and much effort on creating a painting or a sculpture, the viewer was then allowed to consume this work without effort and with one glance. This explains the traditional superiority of the consumer, the viewer, the collector over the artist-craftsperson as a supplier of paintings and sculptures which had to be produced through arduous physical labor. It was not until the introduction of photography and the readymade technique that the artist placed himself on the same level with the viewer in terms of temporal economy, as this also enables the artist to produce images almost immediately. But now the digital camera, which can produce moving images, can also record and distribute these images automatically, without the artist having to spend any time doing so. This gives the artist a clear time surplus:

The viewer now has to spend more time viewing the images than the artist has to produce them. And again: This is not an intentionally lengthened duration of contemplation that the viewer needs to "understand" the image—as the viewer is completely in charge of the duration of conscious contemplation. Rather it is the time a viewer needs to even be able to watch video material in its entirety—and the contemporary technique allows producing a video work of considerable length in a very short time. That is why the basic experience had by the viewer of a video installation is thus the experience of the non-identity and even nonvisibility of the exhibited work. Each time someone visits a video exhibition, he or she is potentially confronted with another clip from the same video, which means that the work is different each time—and at the same time partially eludes the viewer's eye, makes itself invisible.

The non-identity of video images also presents itself at another, as it were, deeper technical level. As has already been said: If one changes certain technical parameters, one also changes the image. Can one perhaps preserve something of the old technology so that the image remains self-identical through all the instances of its display? But to preserve the original technology shifts the perception of a specific image from the image itself to the technical conditions under which it was produced. What we primarily react to is the old-fashioned photographic or video recording technology that becomes apparent when we look at old photographs or videos. The artist did not originally intend to produce this effect, however, as he lacked the possibility of comparing his work with the products of later technological developments.

Thus the image itself may possibly be overlooked if it is reproduced using the original technology. And so the decision becomes understandable to transfer this image to new technological media, to new software and hardware, so that it may look fresh again, so that it becomes interesting not merely in retrospect, but rather appears to be a contemporary image. With this line of argumentation, however, one gets caught in the same dilemma out of which, as is generally known, contemporary theater is unable to extricate itself. Because no one knows what is better: to reveal the epoch or the individuality of the play by the means of its performance. But it is unavoidable that every performance reveals one of these parameters by obscuring the other one. However, one can also use the technical constraints productively—one can play with the technical quality of a digital image on all levels, including the material quality of the monitor or the projection surface, the external light, which as we know substantially changes the viewer's perception of a video image. Thus each presentation of a digitalized image becomes a re-creation of the image.

This shows again: There is no such thing as a copy. In the world of digitalized images, we are dealing only with originals—only with original presentations of the absent, invisible digital original. The exhibition makes copying reversible: It transforms a copy into an original. But this original remains partially invisible and non-identical. Now it becomes clear why it makes sense to apply both cures to the image—to digitalize it and to curate it, to exhibit it. This double medicine is not more effective than the two cures taken separately; it does not make the image truly strong. Quite the contrary: By applying this double medicine one becomes aware of the zones of the invisibility, of one's own lack of visual control, of the impossibility of stabilizing the identity of the image—of which one is not so much aware if he or she is dealing only with the objects in the exhibition space or the freely circulating digitalized images. But that means that the contemporary, postdigital curatorial practice can do something that the traditional exhibition could do only metaphorically: exhibit the Invisible.

Multiple Authorship

Maybe there is no death as we know it. Just documents changing hands.

—Don DeLillo, *White Noise*

For a long time the social function of the exhibition was firmly fixed: the artist produced artworks, which were then either selected and exhibited by the curator of an exhibition, or rejected. The artist was considered an autonomous author. The curator of the exhibition, by contrast, was someone who mediated between the author and the public but was not an author himself. Thus the respective roles of artist and curator were clearly distinct: the artist was concerned with creation; the curator, with selection. The curator could only choose from the store of works that various artists had already produced. That meant that creation was considered primary, and selection, secondary. Accordingly, the inevitable conflict between artist and curator was seen and treated as a conflict between authorship and mediation, between individual and institution, between primary and secondary. That era, however, is now definitively over. The relationship between artist and curator has undergone a fundamental change. Although this change has not resolved the old conflicts, they have taken on a completely different form.

It is simple to state why this situation changed: art today is defined by an identity between creation and selection. At least since Duchamp, it has been the case that selecting an artwork is the same as creating an artwork. That, of course, does not mean that all art since then has become readymade art. It does mean, however, that the creative act has become the act of selection: since Duchamp, producing an object is no longer sufficient for its producer to be considered an artist. One must also select the object one has made oneself and declare it an artwork. Accordingly, since Duchamp there is no longer any difference between an object one produces oneself and one produced by someone else—both have to be selected in order to be considered artworks. Today an author is someone who selects, who authorizes. Since

Duchamp the author has become a curator. The artist is primarily the curator of himself, because he selects his own art. And he also selects others: other objects, other artists. At least since the 1960s artists have created installations in order to demonstrate their personal practices of selection. The installations, however, are nothing other than exhibitions curated by artists, in which objects made by others may be—and are—represented as well as objects made by the artist. Accordingly, however, curators are also freed of the duty to exhibit only those objects that are preselected by the artists. Curators today feel free to combine art objects selected and signed by artists with objects that are taken directly from "life." In short, once the identity between creation and selection has been established, the roles of the artist and of the curator also become identical. A distinction between the (curated) exhibition and the (artistic) installation is still commonly made, but it is essentially obsolete.

The old question must therefore be asked anew: What is an artwork? The answer that present-day art practices offer to this question is straightforward: the artwork is an exhibited object. The object that is not exhibited is not an artwork but merely an object that has the potential to be exhibited as an artwork. Not by chance do we speak of art today as "contemporary art." It is art that must currently be exhibited in order to be considered art at all. The elementary unit of art today is therefore no longer an artwork as object but an art space in which objects are exhibited: the space of an exhibition, of an installation. Present-day art is not the sum of particular things but the topology of particular places. The installation has thus established an extremely voracious form of art that assimilates all other traditional art forms: paintings, drawings, photographs, texts, objects, readymades, films, and recordings. All these art objects are arranged by an artist or curator in the space, according to an order that is purely private, individual, and subjective. Thus the artist or curator has a chance to demonstrate publicly his private, sovereign strategy of selection.

The installation is often denied the status of art because the question arises of what the medium of an installation is. This question arises because traditional art media are all defined according to the specific support of the medium: canvas, stone, or film. The medium of an installation is the space itself; and that means, among other things, that the installation is by no means "immaterial." Quite the contrary: The installation is by all means material, because it is spatial. The installation demonstrates the material of the civilization in which we live particularly well, since it *installs* everything that otherwise merely *circulates* in our civilization. Hence the installation demonstrates the civilizational hardware that otherwise remains unnoticed behind the surface of circulation in the media. And it also shows the artist's sovereignty at work: how this sovereignty defines and practices its strategies of selection. That is why the installation is not a representation of the relationships among things as regulated by economic and other social orders; quite the contrary, the installation offers an opportunity to use the explicit introduction of subjective orders and relations among things in order to call into question at least those orders that must be supposed to exist "out there" in reality.

We must take this opportunity to clear up a misunderstanding that has recently come up again and again in the relevant literature. It has been argued with some insistence that art has reached its end today; and that therefore a new field—visual studies—should take the place of art history. Visual studies is supposed to extend the field of pictorial analysis: rather than considering artistic images exclusively, it is supposed to address the purportedly larger, more open space of all existing images, and to transgress courageously the limits of the old concept of art. The courage to transgress old limits is certainly always impressive and welcome. In this case, however, what seems to be a transgression of limits turns out not to be an extension at all but rather a scaling down of the relevant spaces. As we have noted, art consists not of images but of all possible objects, including utilitarian objects, texts, and so on. And there are no distinct "artistic images"; rather, any image can be used in an artistic context. Turning art history into visual studies is thus not an extension of its field of study but a drastic reduction of it, since it restricts art to what can be considered an "image" in the traditional sense. By contrast, everything that can be presented in an installation space belongs to the realm of the visual arts. In that sense, an individual image is also an installation; it is simply an installation that has been reduced to a single image. The installation is thus not an alternative to the image but precisely the extension of the concept of the image that is lost if the traditional concept of the image is readopted. If we want to extend the concept of the image, it is precisely the installation that we need to discuss, since it defines the universal rules for space by which all images and nonimages must function as spatial objects. In more than one respect the transition to the installation as the guiding form of contemporary art changes the definition of what we define as a work of art. The most significant and far-reaching change is to our understanding of authorship in art.

Increasingly today, we protest against the traditional cult of artistic subjectivity, against the figure of the author, and against the authorial signature. This rebellion usually sees itself as a revolt against the power structures of the system of art that find their visible expression in the figure of the sovereign author. Again and again, critics try to demonstrate that there is no such thing as artistic genius, and consequently that the authorial status of the artist in question cannot be derived from the supposed fact that he is a genius. Rather, the attribution of authorship is seen as a convention used by the institution of art, the art market, and art critics to build up stars strategically and so to profit from them commercially. The struggle against the figure of the author is thus understood as a struggle against an undemocratic system of arbitrary privileges and unfounded hierarchies that historically have represented base commercial interests. Naturally this rebellion against the figure of the author ends with the critics of authorship being declared famous authors, precisely because they have stripped the traditional figure of the author of its power. At first glance, we might see this as merely the well-known process of regicide, in which the king's murderer is made the new king. It is not so simple, however. Rather, this polemic reflects on real processes that take place in the art world but that have yet to be adequately analyzed.

The traditional, sovereign authorship of an individual artist has de facto disappeared; hence it really does not make much sense to rebel against such authorship. When confronted with an art exhibition, we are dealing with multiple authorship. And in fact every art exhibition exhibits something that was selected by one or more artists—from their own production and/or from the mass of readymades. These objects selected by the artists are then selected in turn by one or more curators, who thus also share authorial responsibility for the definitive selection. In addition, these curators are selected and financed by a commission, a foundation, or an institution; thus these commissions, foundations, and institutions also bear authorial and artistic responsibility for the end result. The selected objects are presented in a space selected for the purpose; the choice of such a space, which can lie inside or outside the spaces of an institution, often plays a crucial role in the result. The choice of the space thus also belongs to the artistic, creative process; the same is true of the choice of the architecture of the space by the architect responsible and the choice of the architect by the committees responsible. One could extend at will this list of authorial, artistic decisions that, taken together, result in an exhibition taking one form or another.

If the choice, the selection, and the decision with respect to the exhibition of an object are thus to be acknowledged as acts of artistic creation, then every individual exhibition is the result of many such processes of decision, choice, and selection. From this circumstance result multiple, disparate, heterogeneous authorships that combine, overlap, and intersect, without it being possible to reduce them to an individual, sovereign authorship. This overlapping of multilayered, heterogeneous authorships is characteristic of any larger exhibition of recent years; and with time it becomes clearer and clearer. For example, at a recent Venice Biennale several curators were invited to present their own exhibitions within the framework of a larger exhibition. Thus the result was a hybrid form between a curated exhibition and an artistic installation: the invited curators appeared before the public as artists. But it is also frequently the case that individual artists integrate works by their colleagues in their own installations and thus they appear in public as curators. Consequently, authorial praxis as it functions in the context of art today is increasingly like that of film, music, and theater. The authorship of a film, theatrical production, or a concert is also a multiple one; it is divided among writers, composers, directors, actors, camera operators, conductors, and many other participants. And the producers should by no means be forgotten. The long list of participants that appears at the end of a film, as the viewers gradually begin to leave their seats and make their way to the exit, manifests the fate of authorship in our age, something the art system cannot escape.

Under this new regime of authorship the artist is no longer judged by the objects he has produced but by the exhibitions and projects in which he has participated. Getting to know an artist today means reading his curriculum vitae, not looking at his paintings. His authorship is presumed to be only a partial one. Accordingly, he is measured not by his products but by his participation in the important exhibitions, just as an actor is judged by which roles he has played in which productions and which films. Even when one visits an artist's studio to get to know his oeuvre, one is generally shown a CD-ROM documenting the exhibitions and events in which the artist participated but also documenting the exhibitions, events, projects, and installations that were planned but never realized. This typical experience of a studio visit today demonstrates how the status of the artwork has changed with respect to the new determination of authorship. The unexhibited artwork has ceased to be an artwork; instead, it has become art documentation. These documentations refer either to an exhibition that did indeed take place or to a project for a future exhibition. And that is the crucial aspect: the artwork today does not manifest art; it merely promises art. Art is manifested only in the exhibition, as in fact the title *Manifesta* already states. As long as an object is not yet exhibited and as soon as it is no longer exhibited, it can no longer be considered an artwork. It is either a memory of past art or a promise of future art, but from either perspective it is simply art documentation.

The function of the museum is also modified thereby. Previously the museum functioned just as it does today, namely, as a public archive. But it was an archive of a special kind. The typical historical archive contains documents that refer exclusively to past events; it presumes the ephemerality, the mortality of the life it documents. And indeed the immortal does not need to be documented; only the mortal does. The assumption about the traditional museum, by contrast, was that it contained artworks that possess an eternal artistic value, that embodied art for all times equally, and that can fascinate and convince the present-day viewer as well. That is to say, they did not just document the past but could manifest and emanate art as such here and now. The traditional museum thus functioned as a paradoxical archive of eternal presence, of profane immortality; and in this it was quite distinct from other historical and cultural archives. The material supports of art—canvas, paper, and film—may be considered ephemeral, but art itself is eternally valid.

The museum today, by contrast, is increasingly similar to other archives, since the art documentation that the museum collects does not necessarily appear before the public as art. The permanent exhibition of the museum is no longer—or at least less frequently—presented as a stable, permanent exhibition. Instead, the museum is increasingly a place where temporary exhibitions are shown. The unity of collecting and exhibiting that defined the particular nature of the traditional museum has thus broken down. The museum collection today is seen as documentary raw material that the curator can use in combination with an exhibition program he has developed to express his individual attitude, his individual strategy for dealing with art. Alongside the curator, however, the artist also has the opportunity to shape museum spaces in whole or in part according to his own personal taste. Under these conditions the museum is transformed into a depot, into an archive of artistic documentation that is no longer essentially different from any other form of documentation, and also into a public site for the execution of private artistic projects. As such a site the museum differs from any other site primarily in its design, in its architecture. It is no coincidence that in recent years attention has shifted from the museum collection to museum architecture.

Nevertheless, the museum today has not abandoned entirely its promise of profane immortality. The art documentation that is collected in museums and other art institutions can always be exhibited anew as art. This distinguishes the art projects collected in museums from the life projects documented in other archives: realizing art as art means exhibiting it. And the museum can do that. It is, admittedly, possible to present a life project anew in a reality outside the museum, but only if it itself ultimately concerns an artistic project. This kind of rediscovery of art documentation is, however, only possible because it continues the focus on multiple authorship. Old art documents are restored, transferred to other media, rearranged, installed, and presented in other spaces. Under such conditions it is meaningless to speak of an individual, intact authorship. The artwork as exhibited art documentation is kept alive because its multiple authorships continue to multiply and proliferate; and the site of this proliferation and multiplication of authorship is the present-day museum.

The transformation of the artwork into art documentation by means of its own archiving also enables art today to draw on, in an artistic context, the immense reservoir of documentation of other events and projects that our civilization has collected. And indeed the formulation and documentation of various projects is the main activity of modern man. Whatever one wishes to undertake in business, politics, or culture, the first thing that must be done is to formulate a corresponding project in order to present an application for the approval or financing of this project to one or more responsible authorities. If this project is rejected in its original form, it is modified so that it can still be accepted. If the project is rejected entirely, one has no choice but to propose a new project in its place. Consequently, every member of our society is constantly occupied with drafting, discussing, and rejecting new projects. Assessments are written; budgets are precisely calculated; commissions are formed; committees are convened; and decisions are made. In the meanwhile, no small number of our contemporaries read nothing other than such project proposals, reports, and budgets. Most of these projects, however, are never realized. The fact that they seem unpromising, difficult to finance, or undesirable in general to one or more experts is sufficient for the whole work of formulating the project to have been in vain.

This work is by no means insubstantial; and the amount of work associated with it grows over time. The project documentation presented to the various committees, commissions, and authorities is designed with increasingly effectiveness and formulated in greater detail in order to impress potential assessors. As a result, the formulation of projects is developing into an autonomous art form whose significance for our society has yet to be adequately understood. Irrespective of whether it is realized or not, every project presents a unique vision of the future that is itself fascinating and instructive. Frequently, however, many of the project proposals that our civilization is constantly producing are lost or simply thrown away after they are rejected. This careless approach to the art form of the project formulation is quite regrettable, really, because it often prevents us from analyzing and understanding the hopes and visions of the future that are invested in these proposals, and these things can say more about our society than anything else. Because within the system of art the exhibition of a document is sufficient to give it life, the art archive is particularly well suited to being the archive of these sorts of projects that were realized at some time in the past or will be realized in the future, but above all to being the archive of utopian projects that can never be realized fully. These utopian projects that are doomed to failure in the current economic and political reality can be kept alive in art, in that the documentation of these projects constantly changes hands and authors.

The City in the Age of Touristic Reproduction

Cities originally came about as projects for the future: People moved from the country into the city in order to escape the ancient forces of nature and to build a new future that they could shape and control themselves. The entire course of human history until the present has been defined by this movement from the country into the city—a dynamic to which history in fact owes its direction. Although life in the country has repeatedly been stylized as the golden era of harmony and "natural" contentment, such embellished memories of a life spent in nature have never restrained people from continuing on their chosen historical path. In this respect, the city per se possesses an intrinsically utopian dimension by virtue of being situated outside the natural order. The city is located in the *ou-topos*. City walls once delineated the place where a city was built, clearly designating its utopian—*ou-topian*—character. Indeed, the more utopian a city was signaled to be, the harder it was made to reach and enter this city, be it the Tibetan city of Lhasa, the celestial city of Jerusalem, or Shambala in India. Traditionally cities isolated themselves from the rest of the world in order to make their own way into the future. So, a genuine city is not only utopian, it is also antitourist: it dissociates itself from space as it moves through time.

The struggle with nature, of course, did not cease inside the city either. At the beginning of his *Discourse on Method*, Descartes already observed that since historically evolved cities were not entirely immune to the irrationality of the natural order they would in fact need to be completely demolished if a new, rational, and consummate city were to be erected on the vacated site.[1] Later on, Le Corbusier called for the demolition of Paris to make way for a new rational city to be built in its place. Hence the utopian dream of the total rationality, transparency, and controllability of an urban environment unleashed a historical dynamism that is manifested in the perpetual transformation of all realms of urban life: the quest for utopia forces the city into a permanent process of surpassing and destroying itself—which is why the city has become the natural venue for revolutions, upheavals, constant new beginnings, fleeting fashions, and incessantly changing lifestyles. Built as a haven of security the city soon became the stage for criminality, instability, destruction, anarchy, and terrorism. Accordingly the city presents itself as a blend of utopia and dystopia, whereby modernity undoubtedly cherishes and applauds its dystopian rather than its utopian aspects—urban decadence, danger, and haunting eeriness. This city of eternal ephemerality has frequently been depicted in literature and staged in the cinema: this is the city we know, for instance, from *Blade Runner* or *Terminator I* and *II*, where permission is constantly being given for everything to be blown up or razed to the ground, simply because people are tirelessly engaged in the endeavor to clear a space for what is expected to happen next, for future developments. And over and over again the arrival of the future is impeded and delayed because the remains of the city's previously built fabric can never be fully removed, making it forever impossible to complete the current preparation phase. If indeed anything of any permanence exists in our cities, it is ultimately only to be found in such incessant preparations for the building of something that promises to last a long time; it is in the perpetual postponement of a final solution, the never-ending adjustments, the eternal repairs, and the constantly piecemeal adaptation to new constraints.

In modern times, however, this utopian impulse, the quest for an ideal city, has grown progressively weaker and gradually been supplanted by the fascination of tourism. Today, when we cease to be satisfied with the life that is offered to us in our own city, we no longer strive to change, revolutionize, or rebuild it; instead, we simply move to another city—for a short period or forever—in search of what we miss in our home city. Mobility between cities—in all shades of tourism and migration—has radically altered our relationship to the city as well as the cities themselves. Globalization and mobility have fundamentally called the utopian character of the city into question by reinscribing the urban *ou-topos* into the topography of globalized space. It is no coincidence that in his reflections on this globalized world McLuhan coined the term "global village"—as opposed to global city. For the tourist and the migrant alike, it is the countryside in which the city stands that has once more become the key issue.

It was primarily the first phase of modern tourism—which I will now term romantic tourism—that spawned a distinctly antiutopian attitude toward the city. Romantic tourism in its nineteenth-century guise cast a certain paralysis over the city that had come to be commonly viewed as an aggregate of tourist attractions. The romantic tourist is not in search of universal utopian models but of cultural differences and local identities. His gaze is not utopian but conservative—directed not at the future but at past provenance. Romantic tourism is a machine designed to transform temporariness into permanence, fleetingness into timelessness, ephemerality into monumentality. When a tourist passes through a city, the place is exposed to his gaze as something that lacks history, that is eternal, amounting to a sum of edifices that have always been there and will always remain as they are at the very moment of his arrival, for the tourist is unable to keep track of a city's historical transformation or to perceive the utopian impulse propelling the city into the future. So it can be said that romantic tourism abolishes utopia precisely by bringing us to see it as fulfilled. The touristic gaze romanticizes, monumentalizes, and eternalizes everything that comes within its range. In turn, the city adapts to this materialized utopia, to the medusan gaze of the romantic tourist.

A city's monuments, after all, have not always been standing there simply waiting for tourists to see them; instead, it was tourism that created these monuments. It is tourism that monumentalizes a city: the gaze of the passing tourist transforms the relentlessly fluid, incessantly changing urban life into a monumental image of eternity. The growing volume of tourism also speeds up the process of monumentalization.

We are now witnesses to a sheer explosion of eternity or, to put it more succinctly, of eternalization in our cities. It is no longer only such famed monuments as the Eiffel Tower or Cologne Cathedral that seem to cry out for preservation, but in fact anything that sparks a sense of familiarity in us—after all, that's how things always used to be and that's how they will stay. Even when you go, for example, to New York and visit the South Bronx and see drug dealers shooting each other (or at least looking as if they are about to shoot each other), such scenes are imbued with the dignified aura of monumentality. The first thing that strikes you is, yes, that's how things always used to be here and that's how they will stay—all these colorful types, the picturesque city ruins and danger looming at every corner. At a later date, you might read in the papers that this district is due to be "gentrified," and your reaction would be one of shock and sadness, similar to what you would feel on hearing that Cologne Cathedral or the Eiffel Tower were to be demolished to make way for a department store. You think, here is a slice of authentic, unique, and different life that is going to be destroyed, and once again everything is about to be flattened and rendered banal; what was once monumental and eternal is soon to be irrevocably lost. But such mourning would be premature. For on your next visit to the now gentrified area, you say: how marvelously insipid, ugly, and banal everything is here—it clearly must have always been as insipid as this, and will always remain so. With this the area is instantly remonumentalized—because on one's travels everyday-ness and banality are always experienced as being equally monumental as that which is aesthetically exceptional. Rather than being guided by some intrinsic quality pertaining to a monument, our sense of monumentality is derived from the relentless process of monumentalization, demonumentalization, and remonumentalization that is unleashed by the romantic tourist's gaze.

Incidentally, it was Kant—in his theory of the sublime in *Critique of Judgment*—who first philosophically assessed the figure of the globally roaming tourist in search of aesthetic experiences. He describes the romantic tourist as someone who perceives even his own demise as a possible travel destination and possesses the capacity to experience it as a sublime event. As examples of mathematical sublimity Kant cites mountains or oceans, phenomena that appear to dwarf normal human proportions. As instances of dynamic sublimity he offers colossal natural events such as storms, volcanic eruptions, and other catastrophes whose overpowering force directly threatens our lives. Yet as destinations visited by the romantic tourist, these threats are not in themselves sublime—just as urban monuments are not intrinsically monumental. According to Kant sublimity lies not in "anything in nature" but in the "capacity we have within us" to judge and enjoy without fear the very things that threaten us.[2] Hence the subject of Kant's infinite ideas of reason is the tourist who repeatedly embarks on journeys in search of the extraordinary of enormity and danger in order to confirm his own superiority and sublimity in regard to nature. But in another section of this treatise Kant also points out that, for instance, the inhabitants of the Alps, who have spent their entire lives in the mountains, by no means regard them as sublime, and "without hesitation" consider "all worshipers of icy peaks to be fools."[3] Indeed, in Kant's age the romantic tourist's gaze still differed radically from that of the mountain dweller. With his globalized gaze the tourist views the figure of the Swiss peasant, for instance, as a feature of the landscape—and thereby this figure does not disturb him. To the Swiss peasant kept busy by and taking care of his immediate surroundings the romantic tourist is simply a fool, an idiot he is unable to take seriously. But in the meantime, as we well know, this situation has again completely changed. Even though the inhabitants of any particular region might still regard internationally roaming tourists as fools, nonetheless they increasingly sense the need—no doubt for economic reasons—to assimilate the globalized gaze pointed at them and to adjust their own way of life to the aesthetic predilections of their visitors, the travelers and tourists. And besides, mountain dwellers have now also started to travel and are becoming tourists too.

The times in which we live are thus an era of postromantic, that is, comfortable and total, tourism, marking a new phase in the history of the relations between the urban *ou-topos* and the world's topography. This new phase is in fact not hard to characterize: rather than the individual romantic tourist, it is instead all manner of people, things, signs, and images drawn from all kinds of local cultures that are now leaving their places of origin and undertaking journeys around the world. The rigid distinction between romantic world travelers and a locally based, sedentary population is rapidly being erased. Cities are no longer waiting for the arrival of the tourist—they too are starting to join global circulation, to reproduce themselves on a world scale and to expand in all directions. As they do so, their movement and proliferation are happening at a much faster pace than the individual romantic tourist was ever capable of. This fact prompts the widespread outcry that all cities now increasingly resemble one another and are beginning to homogenize, with the result that when a tourist arrives in a new city he ends up seeing the same things he encountered in all the other cities. This experience of similarity among all contemporary cities often misleads the observer to assume that the globalization process is erasing local cultural idiosyncrasies, identities, and differences. The truth is not that these distinctions have disappeared, but that they in turn have also embarked on a journey, started to reproduce themselves and to expand.

For quite a while now we have been able to enjoy the delights of Chinese cooking not only in China, but also in New York, Paris, and Dortmund. On speculating in which cultural surroundings Chinese food tastes best, the answer is not necessarily "China." If we go to China today and fail to experience Chinese cities as being exotic, this is by no means simply because these places have been strongly shaped by international modern architecture of Western origin, but also because much of what one witnesses there as "authentically Chinese" has long been familiar to visitors from America or Europe, where such Chinese attributes can be found in any town or city. So, far from becoming extinct, local features have in fact become global. The differences between various cities have turned into inner-city differences. The result is a global world city that has replaced the global village. This world city operates like a reproductive machine that relatively swiftly multiplies any local attribute of one particular city in all other cities around the world. Thus, in the course of time, quite dissimilar cities begin to resemble one another, without any particular city serving as a prototypical model for all the others. As soon as a new strain of rap music emerges in some borough of New York it promptly begins to influence the music scene of other cities—just as each new sect in India multiplies and spreads its ashrams throughout the entire world.

But above all, it is today's artists and intellectuals who are spending most of their time in transit—rushing from one exhibition to the next, from one project to another, from one lecture to the next, or from one local cultural context to another. All active participants in today's cultural world are now expected to offer their productive output to a global audience, to be prepared to be constantly on the move from one venue to the next, and to present their work with equal persuasion—regardless of where they are. A life spent in transit like this is bound up with equal degrees of hope and fear. On the one hand, artists are now given the possibility of evading the pressure of prevailing local tastes in a relatively painless way. Thanks to modern means of communication they can seek out like-minded associates from all over the world instead of having to adjust to the tastes and cultural orientation of their immediate surroundings. This, incidentally, also explains the somewhat depoliticized condition of contemporary art that is so frequently deplored. In former times artists compensated for the lack of response to their work among people of their own culture by projecting their aspirations largely on the future, dreaming of political changes that would one day spawn a more appreciative viewer of their work. Today the utopian impulse has shifted direction—acknowledgment is no longer sought in time, but in space: Globalization has replaced the future as the site of utopia. So, rather than practicing avant-garde politics based on the future, we now embrace the politics of travel, migration, and nomadic life, paradoxically rekindling the utopian dimension that had ostensibly died out in the era of romantic tourism.

This means that as travelers we are now observers, not so much of various local settings as of our fellow travelers, all caught up in a permanent global journey that has become identical with life in the world city. Moreover, present-day urban architecture has now begun to move faster than its viewers. This architecture is almost always already there before the tourists arrive. In the race between tourists and architecture it is now the tourist who loses. Although the tourist is annoyed to encounter the same architecture everywhere he goes, he is also amazed to see how successful a certain type of architecture has proved to be in a wide range of disparate cultural settings. We are now prepared to be attracted and persuaded particularly by artistic strategies capable of producing art that achieves the same degree of success regardless of the cultural context and conditions in which it is viewed. What fascinates us nowadays is precisely not locally defined differences and cultural identities but artistic forms that persistently manage to assert their own specific identity and integrity wherever they are presented. Since we have all become tourists capable only of observing other tourists, what especially impresses us about all things, customs, and practices is their capacity for reproduction, dissemination, self-preservation, and survival under the most diverse local conditions.

With this, the strategies of postromantic, total tourism are now supplanting the old strategies of utopia and enlightenment. Redundant architectural and artistic styles, political prejudices, religious myths, and traditional customs are no longer meant to be transcended in the name of universality but to be touristically reproduced and globally disseminated. Today's world city is homogenous without being universal. It was formerly believed that attaining the universality of ideas and creativity depended on the individual transcending his own local traditions in the name of universal validity. Consequently, the utopia hailed by the radical avant-garde was reductive: one was first expected to aspire to a pure, elemental form stripped of all historical and local traits in order to claim its universal and global validity. This too was how classical modernist art proceeded—first reduce something to its essence, then spread it around the world. Today's art and architecture, by contrast, are globally disseminated without even first bothering with any such reduction to some universally valid essence. The possibilities of global networking, mobility, reproduction, and distribution have rendered traditional calls for the universality of form or content utterly obsolete. Nowadays any cultural phenomenon can proliferate without being required to make claims for its own universality. Universal thinking is being supplanted by the universal media dissemination of any kind of local ideas whatsoever. The universality of artistic form is being displaced by the global reproduction of any kind of local form whatsoever. As a result, while today's viewers are constantly confronted with the same urban surroundings, it is impossible to say whether the character of these surroundings is in any sense "universal." In the postmodernist period, all architecture following in the footsteps of Bauhaus was criticized for being monotonous and reductive—as architecture that first leveled and then erased all local identities. But today the whole plethora of local styles is spreading at the same global pace as the international style once did on its own.

Thus as a consequence of total tourism we are now witnessing the emergence of a homogeneity bereft of all universality, an utterly new and up-to-date development. Accordingly, in the context of total tourism we once more encounter a utopia, but one that differs radically from the static, immobile utopia of the city that demarcates itself from the remaining topography and is segregated from the rest of the country. Thus we now all live in a world city where living and traveling have become synonymous, where there is no longer any perceptible difference between the city's residents and its visitors. The utopia of an eternal universal order has been replaced by the utopia of constant global mobility. In turn, the dystopian dimension of this utopia has also changed—terrorist cells and designer drugs now proliferate in cities all around the world at the same pace as, say, Prada boutiques.

Interestingly, as early as the beginning of the twentieth century several radical utopians in the Russian avant-garde put forward plans for future cities where all apartments and houses would be, first, uniform in design and, second, mobile. In an astonishing manner their designs made the touristic journey synonymous with its destination. In a similar vein the poet Velimir Khlebnikov proposed that all inhabitants of Russia be lodged inside glass cells mounted on wheels, allowing them to travel freely everywhere and to see everything, but without in any way obstructing their visibility to others. With this, the tourist and the city dweller become identical—and all the tourist is capable of seeing is other tourists. Incidentally, Kazimir Malevich took Khlebnikov's project one step further when he suggested placing every single person inside an individual cosmic vessel to keep him constantly floating in space and to allow him to fly from one planet to the next. His proposal would irrevocably turn the human subject into an eternal tourist on a never-ending journey whereby—insulated within his very own, yet always identical cell—he would become a monument in himself. We encounter an analogous vision in the popular TV series *Star Trek*, where the spaceship *Enterprise* has become a constantly moving, utopian, monumental space that never alters throughout all this series' countless episodes, even though—or precisely because—it is always moving at the speed of light. In this instance, utopia pursues the strategy of transcending the antagonism between immobility and traveling; between sedentary and nomadic life, between comfort and danger, between the city and the countryside—as the creation of a total space in which the topography of the Earth's surface becomes identical with the *ou-topos* of the eternal city.

In a striking fashion, such a utopian transcendence of nature was already being considered in the period of German Romanticism. Evidence of this can be found in a passage in *Ästetik des Hässlichen* (The aesthetics of the ugly) (1853) written by the Hegel disciple, Karl Rosenkranz:

> Take, for example, our Earth which, in order to be beautiful as a body, would need to be a perfect sphere. But it is not. It is flattened at both poles and swollen around the equator, besides which the elevations of its surface are extremely uneven. From a purely stereometric point of view, the profile of the Earth's crust reveals to us the most haphazard confusion of elevations and depressions with all manner of incalculable contours. Hence, where the surface of the Moon with its disarray of heights and depths is concerned, we are equally unable to state whether it is beautiful, etc.[4]

At the time this was written humankind was technologically still far removed from the possibility of space travel. Here, altogether in the spirit of an avant-garde utopia or a sci-fi movie, the agent of global aesthetic contemplation is nonetheless depicted as an alien that has just arrived from outer space and then, observing from a comfortable distance, formed an aesthetic judgment of our galaxy's appearance. Of course, this alien is imputed to have distinctly classical tastes, which is why it fails to consider our planet and its immediate surroundings as especially beautiful. But regardless of the alien's final aesthetic judgment, one thing is clear: this is a first manifestation of the gaze of the consummate urban dweller who, constantly in motion in the *ou-topos* of black cosmic space, peers down at the topography of our world from a touristic, aesthetic distance.

Critical Reflections

For some time now, the art critic has seemed a legitimate representative of the art world. Like the artist, curator, gallery owner, and collector, when an art critic shows up at an opening or some other art-world event, nobody wonders, What's he doing here? That something should be written about art is taken as self-evident. When works of art aren't provided with a text—in an accompanying pamphlet, catalog, art magazine, or elsewhere—they seem to have been delivered into the world unprotected, lost and unclad. Images without text are embarrassing, like a naked person in a public space. At the very least they need a textual bikini in the form of an inscription with the name of the artist and the title (in the worst case this can read "Untitled"). Only the domestic intimacy of a private collection allows for the full naked-ness of a work of art.

The function of the art critic—perhaps "art commentator" would be a better way of putting it—consists, it is thought, in preparing such protective text-clothes for works of art. These are, from the start, texts not necessarily written to be read. The art commentator's role is entirely misconstrued if one expects him to be clear and comprehensible. In fact, the more hermetic and opaque a text, the better: Texts that are too see-through let works of art come across naked. Of course, there are those whose transparency is so absolute that the effect is especially opaque. Such texts provide the best protection, a trick well known to every fashion designer. In any case, it would be naive for anyone to try to read art commentary. Luckily, few in the art world have hit upon this idea.

Thus, art commentary finds itself today in a confusing position, at once indispensable and superfluous. Other than its sheer material presence, one doesn't really know what to expect of it or desire from it. This confusion is rooted in the genealogy of contemporary criticism: The positioning of the critic within the art world is anything but self-evident. As is generally known, the figure of the art critic emerged at the end of the eighteenth and beginning of the nineteenth century, alongside the gradual rise of a broad, democratic public. At that time, he was certainly not regarded as a representative of the art world but strictly as an outside observer whose function was to judge and criticize works of art in the name of the public exactly as would any other well-educated observer with the time and literary facility: Good taste was seen as the expression of an aesthetic "common sense." The art critic's judgment should be incorruptible, that is, bear no obligation to the artist. For a critic to give up his distance meant being corrupted by the art world and neglecting his professional responsibilities: This demand for disinterested art criticism in the name of the public sphere is the assertion of Kant's third critique, the first truly important aesthetic treatise of modernity.

The judicial ideal, however, was betrayed by the art criticism of the historical avant-garde. The art of the avant-garde consciously withdrew itself from the judgment of the public. It did not address the public as it was but instead spoke to a new humanity as it should—or at least could—be. The art of the avant-garde presupposed a different, new humanity for its reception—one that would be able to grasp the hidden meaning of pure color and form (Kandinsky), to subject its imagination and even its daily life to the strict laws of geometry (Malevich, Mondrian, the Constructivists, Bauhaus), to recognize a urinal as a work of art (Duchamp). The avant-garde thus introduced a rupture in society not reducible to any previously existing social differences.

The new, artificial difference is the true artwork of the avant-garde. Now it is not the observer who judges the artwork, but the artwork that judges—and often condemns—its public. This strategy has often been called elitist, but it suggests an elite equally open to anyone insofar as it excludes everyone to the same degree. To be chosen doesn't automatically mean dominance, or even mastery. Every individual is free to place himself, against the rest of the public, on the side of the artwork—to number himself among those constituting the new humanity. Several art critics of the historical avant-garde did just that. In place of the critic in the name of society arose social critique in the name of art: The artwork doesn't form the object of judgment but is instead taken as the point of departure for a critique aimed at society and the world.

The art critic of today inherited the older public office along with the avant-garde betrayal of this office. The paradoxical task of judging art in the name of the public while criticizing society in the name of art opens a deep rift within the discourse of contemporary criticism. And one can read today's critical discourse as an attempt to bridge, or at least conceal, this divide. For example, there is the critic's demand that art thematize existing social differences and position itself against the illusion of cultural homogeneity. That certainly sounds very avant-garde, but what one forgets is that the avant-garde didn't thematize already existing differences but introduced previously nonexistent ones. The public was equally bewildered in the face of Malevich's Suprematism and Duchamp's Dadaism, and it is this generalized nonunderstanding—bewilderment regardless of class, race, or gender— that is actually the democratic moment of the various avant-garde projects. These projects were not in a position to suspend existing social differences and thereby create cultural unity, but they were able to introduce distinctions so radical and new that they could overdetermine differences as they stood.

There's nothing wrong in itself with the demand that art give up its modernist "autonomy" and become medium of social critique, but what goes unmentioned is that the critical stance is blunted, banalized, and finally made impossible by this requirement. When art relinquishes its autonomous ability to artificially produce its own differences, it also loses the ability to subject society, as it is, to a radical critique. All that remains for art is to illustrate a critique that society has already leveled at or manufactured for itself. To demand that art be practiced in the name of existing social differences is actually to demand the affirmation of the existing structure of society in the guise of social critique.

In our time art is generally understood as a form of social communication; it is taken as self-evident that all people want to communicate and strive for communicative recognition. Even if the contemporary discourse of art criticism understands the famous "other" not in the sense of particular cultural identities, but as desire, power, libido, the unconscious, the real—art is still interpreted as an attempt to communicate this other, to give it voice and shape. Even if communication is not achieved, the desire for it suffices to secure acceptance. Also the work of the classical avant-garde is accepted when it is understood as subordinate to the earnest intention of bringing the unconscious and the otherness into expression: the incomprehensibility to the average observer of the resulting art is excused by virtue of the impossibility of any communicative mediation of the "radical other."

But this "other" that desires unconditionally to convey itself, that wants to be communicative, is, of course, not other enough. What made the classical avant-garde interesting and radical was precisely that it consciously shunned conventional social communication: it excommunicated itself. The "incomprehensibility" of the avant-garde was not just the effect of a communication breakdown. Language, including visual language, can be used not only as a means of communication but also as a means of strategic discommunication or even self-excommunication, that is, a voluntary departure from the community of the communicating. And this strategy of self-excommunication is absolutely legitimate. One can also wish to erect a linguistic barrier between oneself and the other in order to gain a critical distance from society. And the autonomy of art is nothing other than this movement of self-excommunication. It is a question of attaining power over differences, a question of strategy—instead of overcoming or communicating old differences, new ones are produced.

The departure from social communication repeatedly practiced by modern art has often been described, ironically, as escapism. But every escapism is always followed by a return: Thus the Rousseauian hero first leaves Paris and wanders through forest and meadow only to return to Paris, set up a guillotine in the center of the city, and subject his former superiors and colleagues to a radical critique, that is, cut off their heads. Every revolution worth its salt attempts to replace society as it is with a new, artificial society. The artistic impulse always plays a decisive role here. That so many attempts to produce a new humanity have so far met with disappointment explains many critics' trepidation to put too much hope in the avant-garde. Instead, they want to drive the avant-garde back to the stable ground of facts, fence it in, and tether it to the real, to existent differences.

Still, the question remains: What are these real existing differences? Most are artificial through and through. Technology and fashion generate the important differences of our day. And where they are consciously, strategically produced—whether in high art, design, cinema, pop music, or new media—the tradition of the avant-garde lives on (the recent enthusiasm for the Internet, reminiscent of the time of the classical avant-garde, is a case in point). Social art critics don't go in for such technical or fashionable differences, even though they have the success of such artificial differences to thank for the fact that their brand of discourse is in style (or at least was until fairly recently).

So, many years after the rise of the avant-garde, the discourse of contemporary art theory continues to suffer because artificial, consciously produced differences still remain unprivileged. Just as in the era of the historical avant-garde, those artists introducing artificial, aesthetic differences are reproached for being motivated exclusively by commercial and strategic interests. To react to the fashionable with enthusiasm and hope, to see in it a chance for a new and interesting social difference, is considered "improper" in "serious" theory.

The unwillingness of the critic to identify himself with specific artistic positions is chalked up theoretically to the opinion that we have reached the end of art history. Arthur Danto, for example, argues in *After the End of Art* that those programs of the avant-garde intended to define the essence and function of art have finally become untenable. It is thus no longer possible to privilege a particular kind of art theoretically as those critics who think in an avant-garde mode—in the American context the paradigm remains Clement Greenberg—have again and again tried to do. The development of art in this century has ended in a pluralism that relativizes everything, makes everything possible at all times, and no longer allows for critically grounded judgment. This analysis certainly seems plausible. But today's pluralism is itself artificial through and through—a product of the avant-garde. A single modern work of art is a huge contemporary differentiation machine.

If the critics had not, as Greenberg did, taken specific works of art as the occasion for drawing new lines of demarcation in the field of theory and art politics, we would have no pluralism today, because this artistic pluralism certainly cannot be reduced to an already existing social pluralism. Even the social art critics can make their distinctions between the "natural" and the "socially coded" relevant for art criticism only because they place these (artificial) distinctions like readymades in the context of modernist differentiation. And Danto makes the same move as Greenberg when he attempts to draw all the consequences from Warhol's *Brillo Boxes* and to think of this artwork as the beginning of an absolutely new era. Today's pluralism means decisively that no single position can be unequivocally privileged over another. But not all differences between two positions are of equal value; some differences are more interesting than others. It pays to concern oneself with such interesting differences—regardless of which position one advocates. It pays even more to create new, interesting differences that further drive the condition of pluralism. And since these differences are purely artificial, a natural, historical end cannot be attributed to the process of differentiation.

Perhaps the real reason today's art critic no longer passionately champions a particular attitude in art and its relevance for theory and cultural politics is more psychological than theoretical. First, in so doing, the advocating critic feels he is left in the lurch by the artist. One might easily have supposed that after the critic has crossed over to the side of the artist he would have won the artist's gratitude and become his confidante. But it doesn't work this way. The critic's text—so most artists believe—seems less to protect the work from detractors than to isolate it from its potential admirers. Rigorous theoretical definition is bad for business. Thus, many artists protect themselves against theoretical commentary in the hopes that a naked work of art will be more seductive than one dressed in a text. Actually, artists prefer formulations that are as vague as possible: the work is "charged with tension," "critical" (without any indication of how or why); the artist "deconstructs social codes," "puts our habitual way of seeing into question," "practices an elaboration" of something or other. Or artists prefer to speak themselves, to tell their personal histories and demonstrate how everything, even quite trivial objects that fall under their gaze, takes on a deep, personal meaning for them (at many exhibitions, the observer has the feeling of being put in the place of a social worker or psychotherapist without receiving any corresponding financial compensation, an effect often parodied in the installations of Ilya Kabakov and, in a different way, in the video work of Tony Oursler).

On the other hand, the critic's attempts to turn back to the public and offer himself as the defender of its legitimate claims lead to nothing: the old betrayal hasn't been forgiven. The public still regards the critic as an insider, a public-relations agent for the art industry. Ironically, the critic wields the least power of anyone in that industry. When a critic writes for a catalog, it's arranged and paid for by the same people who are exhibiting the artist he's reviewing. When he writes for a journal or newspaper, he is covering an exhibition the reader already assumes is worthy of mention. The critic thus has no real chance to write about an artist if the artist isn't already established; someone else in the art world has already decided that the artist is deserving of a show. One could object that a critic can at least give a negative review. That is certainly true—but it makes no difference. Through these decades of artistic revolutions, movements, and countermovements, the public in this century has finally come around to the position that a negative review is no different from a positive one. What matters in a review is which artists are mentioned where and how long they are discussed. Everything else is everything else.

As a reaction to this situation, a bitter, disappointed, nihilistic tone pervades the art criticism of today, which clearly ruins its style. This is a shame, because the art system is still not such a bad place for a writer. It's true that most of these texts don't get read—but for this very reason one can, in principle, write whatever one wants. Under the pretext of opening up the different contexts of a work of art, the most diverse theories, intellectual takes, rhetorical strategies, stylistic props, scholarly knowledge, personal stories, and examples from all walks of life can be combined in the same text at will—in a way not possible in the two other areas open to writers in our culture, the academy and the mass media. Almost nowhere else does the pure textuality of the text show itself so clearly as in art criticism. The art system protects the writer as much from the demand that he convey some kind of "knowledge" to the masses of students as it does from the competition for readers among those covering the O.J. Simpson trial. The public within the art world is relatively small: the pressure of a broad public forum is missing. Therefore, the text need not meet with the concurrence of this public. Of course, fashion does emerge as a consideration—sometimes one should sense authenticity in an artwork, at other times perceive that there is no authenticity, sometimes emphasize political relevance, at other times slip into private obsessions—but not a strict one. There are always those who don't like the prevailing fashion because they liked an earlier one, or because they're hoping for the next, or both.

But above all, the art critic cannot err. Of course, the critic comes under repeated accusation of having misjudged or misinterpreted a particular art form. But this reproach is unfounded. A biologist can err, for instance, if he describes an alligator as being other than an alligator is, because alligators don't read critical texts and therefore their behavior is not influenced by them. The artist, in contrast, can adapt his work to the judgment and theoretical approach of the critic. When a gap arises between the work of the artist and the judgment of the critic, one cannot necessarily say that the critic misjudged the artist. Maybe the artist misread the critic? But that's not so bad, either:

The next artist might read him better. It would be false to think somehow that Baudelaire overrated Constantin Guys, or Greenberg Jules Olitski, because the theoretical excess the two produced has its own value and can stimulate other artists.

It's also not that important which artworks the art critic uses to illustrate his theoretically generated differences. The difference itself is important—and it doesn't appear in the works but in their use, including their interpretation—even if various images seem suited to the purposes of the critic. There is no dearth of useful illustrations; we're observing a tremendous overproduction of images today. (Artists have increasingly recognized this—and begun to write themselves. The production of images serves them more as a cover than as an actual goal.) The relationship between image and text has changed. Before it seemed important to provide a good commentary for a work. Today it seems important to provide a good illustration for a text, which demonstrates that the image with commentary no longer interests us as much as the illustrated text. The art critic's betrayal of the criterion of public taste turned him into an artist. In the process, any claim to a metalevel of judgment was lost. Yet art criticism has long since become an art in its own right; with language as its medium and the broad base of images available, it moves as autocratically as has become the custom in art, cinema, or design. Thus a gradual erasure of the line between artist and art critic completes itself, while the traditional distinction between artist and curator, and critic and curator, tends toward disappearance. Only the new, artificial dividing lines in cultural politics are important, those that are drawn in each individual case, with intention and strategy.

Part II

Art at War

The relationship between art and war, or art and terror, has always been an ambivalent one, to put it mildly. True, art needs peace and quiet for its development. And yet time and time again it has used this quiet, of all things, to sing the praises of war heroes and their heroic deeds. The representation of the glory and suffering of war was for a long time a preferred topic for art. But the artist of the classic age was only a narrator or an illustrator of war events—in the past the artist never competed with the warrior. The division of labor between war and art was quite clear. The warrior did the actual fighting, and the artist represented this fight by narrating it or depicting it.

Thus the warrior and artist were mutually dependent. The artist needed the warrior as a topic for art. But the warrior needed the artist even more. After all, the artist could always find another, more peaceful topic for his or her work. But only an artist was able to bestow fame on the warrior and to secure this fame for generations to come. In a certain sense the heroic war action of the past was futile and irrelevant without the artist, who had the power to witness this heroic action and inscribe it into the memory of humankind. But in our time the situation has changed drastically: The contemporary warrior no longer needs an artist to acquire fame and inscribe his feats into the universal memory. For this purpose the contemporary warrior has all the contemporary media at his immediate disposal. Every act of terror, every act of war is immediately registered, represented, described, depicted, narrated, and interpreted by the media. This machine of media coverage works almost automatically. It requires no individual artistic intervention, no individual artistic decision to be put into motion. By pushing a button that explodes a bomb a contemporary warrior or terrorist pushes a button that starts the media machine.

Indeed, the contemporary mass media has emerged as by far the largest and most powerful machine for producing images—vastly more extensive and effective than our contemporary art system. We are constantly fed images of war, terror, and catastrophes of all kinds, at a level of image production and distribution with which the artist cannot compete. So it seems that the artist—this last craftsperson of present-day modernity—stands no chance of rivaling the supremacy of these commercially driven image-generating machines.

And beyond this, the terrorists and warriors themselves are beginning to act as artists. Video art especially has become the medium of choice for contemporary warriors. Bin Laden is communicating with the outer world primarily by means of this medium: We all know him in the first place as a video artist. The same can be said of the videos representing beheadings, confessions of the terrorists, and the like: In all these cases we have consciously and artistically staged events with their own easily recognizable aesthetics. Here we have warriors who do not wait for an artist to represent their acts of war and terror: Instead, the act of war itself coincides with its documentation, with its representation. The function of art as a medium of representation and the role of the artist as a mediator between reality and memory are here completely eliminated. The same can be said of the famous photographs and videos from the Abu-Ghraib prison in Baghdad. These videos and photographs demonstrate an uncanny aesthetic similarity with alternative, subversive European and American art and filmmaking of the 1960s and '70s. The iconographic and stylistic similarity is, in fact, striking (Viennese Actionism, Pasolini, etc.). In both cases the goal is to reveal a naked, vulnerable, desiring body that is habitually covered by the system of social conventions. But, of course, the subversive art of the '60s and '70s had a goal to undermine the traditional set of beliefs and conventions that were dominating the artist's own culture. In the Abu-Ghraib image production, this goal is, we can safely say, completely perverted. The same subversive aesthetics is used to attack and to undermine a different, other culture in an act of violence, in an act of humiliation of the other (instead of self-questioning including self-humiliation)—leaving the conservative values of the perpetrator's own culture completely unquestioned. But in any case it is worth mentioning that on both sides of the war on terror, image production and distribution is effectuated without any intervention by an artist.

Let us now leave aside all the ethical and political considerations and evaluations of this kind of image production; I believe these considerations are more or less obvious. At the moment it is important for me to state that we are speaking here about the images that became the icons of the contemporary collective imagination. The terrorist videos and the videos from the Abu-Ghraib prison are planted in our consciousness and even subconsciousness much more deeply than any work of any contemporary artist. This elimination of the artist from the practice of image production is especially painful for the art system because, at least since the beginning of modernity, artists have wanted to be radical, daring, taboo-breaking, going beyond all the limitations and borders. The avant-garde art discourse makes use of many concepts from the military sphere, including the notion of the avant-garde itself. There is talk of exploding norms, destroying traditions, violating taboos, practicing certain artistic strategies, attacking the existing institutions, and the like. From this we can see that not only does modern art go along with, illustrate, laud, or criticize war as it did earlier, but also wages war itself. The artists of the classical avant-garde saw themselves as agents of negation, destruction, eradication of all traditional forms of art. In accordance with the famous dictum "negation is creation," which was inspired by the Hegelian dialectic and propagated by authors such as Bakunin and Nietzsche under the title of "active nihilism," avant-garde artists felt themselves empowered to create new icons through destruction of the old ones. A modern work of art was measured by how radical it was, how far the artist had gone in destroying artistic tradition. Although in the meanwhile the modernity itself has often enough been declared passé, to this very day this criterion of radicalness has lost nothing of its relevance to our evaluation of art. The worst thing that can be said of an artist continues to be that his or her art is "harmless."

This means that modern art has a more than ambivalent relationship with violence, with terrorism. An artist's negative reaction to repressive, state-organized power is something that almost goes without saying. Artists who are committed to the tradition of modernity will feel themselves unambiguously compelled by this tradition to defend the individual's sovereignty against state oppression. But the artist's attitude toward individual and revolutionary violence is more complicated, insofar as it also practices a radical affirmation of the individual's sovereignty over the state. There is a long history behind the profound inner complicity between modern art and modern revolutionary, individual violence. In both cases, radical negation is equated with authentic creativity, whether in the area of art or politics. Over and over again this complicity results in a form of rivalry.

Thus art and politics are connected at least in one fundamental respect: both are areas in which a struggle for recognition is being waged. As defined by Alexander Kojève in his commentary on Hegel, this struggle for recognition surpasses the usual struggle for the distribution of material goods, which in modernity is generally regulated by market forces. What is at stake here is not merely that a certain desire be satisfied but that it also be recognized as socially legitimate. Whereas politics is an arena in which various group interests have, both in the past and the present, fought for recognition, artists of the classical avant-garde have already contended for the recognition of all individual forms and artistic procedures that were not previously considered legitimate. In other words, the classical avant-garde has struggled to achieve recognition for all visual signs, forms, and media as the legitimate objects of artistic desire and, hence, also of representation in art. Both forms of struggle are intrinsically bound up with each other, and both have as their aim a situation in which all people with their various interests, as indeed also all forms and artistic procedures, will finally be granted equal rights. And both forms of struggle are thought of, in the context of modernity, as being intrinsically violent.

Along these lines, Don DeLillo writes in his novel *Mao II* that terrorists and writers are engaged in a zero-sum game: by radically negating that which exists, both wish to create a narrative that would be capable of capturing society's imagination—and thereby altering society. In this sense, terrorists and writers are rivals—and, as DeLillo notes, nowadays the writer is beaten hands down because today's media use the terrorists' acts to create a powerful narrative with which no writer can contend. But, of course, this kind of rivalry is even more obvious in the case of the artist than in the case of the writer. The contemporary artist uses the same media as the terrorist: photography, video, film. At the same time it is clear that the artist cannot go further than the terrorist does; the artist cannot compete with the terrorist in the field of radical gesture. In his *Surrealist Manifesto* André Breton famously proclaimed the terrorist act of shooting into a peaceful crowd to be the authentically Surrealist, artistic gesture. Today this gesture seems to be left far behind by recent developments. In terms of the symbolic exchange, operating by the way of potlatch, as it was described by Marcel Mauss or by Georges Bataille, this means that in the rivalry in radicality of destruction and self-destruction, art is obviously on the losing side.

But it seems to me that this very popular way of comparing art and terrorism, or art and war, is fundamentally flawed. And now I will try to show where I see a fallacy. The art of the avant-garde, the art of modernity was iconoclastic. There is no doubt about that. But would we say that terrorism is iconoclastic? No; the terrorist is rather an iconophile. The terrorist's or the warrior's image production has as its goal to produce strong images—images we would tend to accept as being "real," as being "true," as being the "icons" of the hidden, terrible reality that is for us the global political reality of our time. I would say: These images are the icons of the contemporary political theology that dominates our collective imagination. These images draw their power, their persuasiveness from a very effective form of moral blackmail. After so many decades of modern and postmodern criticism of the image, of mimesis, of the representation, we feel ourselves somewhat ashamed by saying that such images of terror or torture are not true, not real. We cannot say that these images are not true, because we know that these images have been paid for by a real loss of life—a loss of life that is documented by these images. Magritte could easily say that a painted apple is not a real apple or that a painted pipe is not a real pipe. But how can we say that a videotaped beheading is not a real beheading? Or that a videotaped ritual of humiliation in the Abu-Ghraib prison is not a real ritual? Thus after many years of the critique of representation directed against the naive belief in photographic and cinematic truth, we are now again ready to accept certain photographed and videotaped images as unquestionably true.

This means: The terrorist, the warrior is radical—but he is not radical in the same sense as the artist is radical. He does not practice iconoclasm. Rather, he wants to reinforce belief in the image, to reinforce the iconophilic seduction, the iconophilic desire. And he takes exceptional, radical measures to end the history of iconoclasm, to end the critique of representation. We are confronted here with a strategy that is historically quite new. Indeed, the traditional warrior was interested in the images that would be able to glorify him, to present him in a favorable, positive, attractive way. And we, of course, have accumulated a long tradition of criticizing, deconstructing such strategies of pictorial idealization. But the pictorial strategy of contemporary warrior is a strategy of shock and awe; it is a pictorial strategy of intimidation. And it is, of course, only possible after the long history of modern art producing images of angst, cruelty, disfiguration. The traditional critique of representation was driven by a suspicion that there must be something ugly and terrifying hidden behind the surface of the conventional idealized image. But the contemporary warrior shows us precisely that—this hidden ugliness, the image of our own suspicion, our own angst.

And precisely because of this we feel ourselves immediately compelled to recognize these images as true. We see that things are as bad as we expected them to be—maybe even worse. Our worst suspicions are confirmed: The hidden reality behind the image is shown to us as ugly as we expected it to be. So we have a feeling that our critical journey has come to its end, that our critical task is completed, that our mission as critical intellectuals is accomplished. Now the truth of the political reveals itself—and we can contemplate the new icons of the contemporary political theology without any need to go further, because these icons are terrible enough by themselves. And so it is sufficient to comment on these icons—it no longer makes sense to criticize them. This explains the macabre fascination that finds its expression in many recent publications dedicated to the images of war on terror that are emerging on the both sides of the invisible front.

That is why I don't believe that the terrorist is a successful rival of the modern artist by being even more radical than the artist. I rather think that the terrorist or the antiterrorist warrior with his embedded image-production machine is the enemy of the modern artist, because he tries to create images that have a claim to be true and real—beyond any criticism of representation. The images of terror and war were in fact proclaimed by many of today's authors as the sign of the return of the real—as visual proof of the end of the critique of the image as it was practiced in the last century. But I think that it is too early to give up this critique. Of course, the images I refer to have some elementary, empirical truth: They document certain events, and their documentary value can be analyzed, investigated, confirmed, or rejected. There are some technical means to establish if a certain image is empirically true or if it is simulated, modified, or falsified. But we have to differentiate between this empirical truth and empirical use of an image as, let us say, judicial evidence, and its symbolic value within the media economy of symbolic exchange.

The images of terror and counterterror that circulate permanently in the networks of the contemporary media and become almost unescapable for a TV viewer are shown primarily not in the context of an empirical, criminal investigation. Their function is to show something more than this or that concrete, empirical incident; they produce the universally valid images of the political sublime. The notion of sublime is associated for us in the first place with its analysis by Kant who used as examples of the sublime images of the Swiss mountains and sea tempests. It is also associated with the essay by Jean-François Lyotard on the relationship between the avant-garde and the sublime. But, actually, the notion of the sublime has its origin in the treatise by Edmund Burke on the notions of the sublime and the beautiful—and there Burke uses as an example of the sublime the public beheadings and tortures that were common in the centuries before the Enlightenment. But we should also not forget that the reign of the Enlightenment itself was introduced by the public exposure of mass beheadings by guillotine in the center of revolutionary Paris.

In his *Phenomenology of Spirit* Hegel writes of this exposure that it created true equality among men because it made perfectly clear that no one can claim any more that his death has any higher meaning. During the nineteth and twentieth centuries the massive depoliticization of the sublime took place. Now we experience the return not of the real but of the political sublime—in the form of the repoliticization of the sublime. Contemporary politics no longer represents itself as beautiful—as even the totalitarian states of the twentieth century still did. Instead, contemporary politics represents itself as sublime again—that is, as ugly, repelling, unbearable, terrifying. And even more: All the political forces of the contemporary world are involved in the increasing production of the political sublime—by competing for the strongest, most terrifying image. It is as if Nazi Germany were to advertise for itself using images of Auschwitz, and the Stalinist Soviet Union using images of the Gulag. Such a strategy is new. But not as new as it seems to be.

The point Burke had originally tried to make is precisely this: a terrifying, sublime image of violence is still merely an image. An image of terror is also produced, staged—and can be aesthetically analyzed and criticized in terms of a critique of representation. This kind of criticism does not indicate any lack of moral sense. The moral sense comes in where it relates to the individual, empirical event that is documented by a certain image. But at the moment an image begins to circulate in the media and acquires the symbolic value of a representation of the political sublime, it can be subjected to art criticism along with every other image. This art criticism can be theoretical. But it can be manifested by the means of art itself—as became a tradition in the context of modernist art. It seems to me that this kind of criticism is already taking place in the art world, but I would rather not name names here because it would distract me from the immediate goal of this essay, which is to diagnose the contemporary regime of image production and distribution as it takes place in the contemporary media. I would only like to point out that the goal of contemporary criticism of representation should be a twofold one. First, this criticism should be directed against all kinds of censorship and suppression of images that would prevent us from being confronted with the reality of war and terror. And this kind of censorship is, of course, still in existence. This kind of censorship, legitimizing itself as the defense of "moral values" and "family rights" can, of course, be applied to the coverage of the wars that takes place today—and demand the sanitization of their representation in the media. But at the same time we are in need of criticism that analyzes the use of these images of violence as the new icons of the political sublime, and that analyzes the symbolic and even commercial competition for the strongest image.

And it seems to me that the context of art is especially appropriate for this second kind of criticism. The art world seems to be very small, closed in, and even irrelevant compared with the power of today's media markets. But in reality, the diversity of images circulating in the media is highly limited compared to the diversity of those circulating in contemporary art. Indeed, to be effectively propagated and exploited in the commercial mass media, images need to be easily recognizable to a broad target audience, which renders the mass media nearly tautological. The variety of images circulating in the mass media is, therefore, vastly more limited than the range of images preserved in museums of modern art or produced by contemporary art.

Since Duchamp, modern art has practiced an elevation of "mere things" to the status of artworks. This upward movement created an illusion that being an artwork is something higher and better than being simply real, being a mere thing. But at the same time modern art went through a long period of self-criticism in the name of reality. The name "art" was used in this context rather as an accusation, as a denigration. To say something is "mere art" is an even greater insult than to say it is a mere object. The equalizing power of modern and contemporary art works both ways—it valorizes and devalorizes at the same time. And this means: To say of the images produced by war and terrorism that on the symbolic level they are merely art is not to elevate or sanctify but to criticize them.

The fascination with images of the political sublime that we can now view almost anywhere can be interpreted as a specific case of nostalgia for the masterpiece, for a true, real image. The media—and not the museum, not the art system—seem now to be the place where such a longing for an over-whelming, immediately persuasive, genuinely strong image is expected to be satisfied. We have here a certain form of a reality show that makes a claim to be a representation of political reality itself—in its most radical forms. But this claim can only be sustained by the fact that we are not able to practice the critique of representation in the context of the contemporary media. The reason for this is quite simple: The media show us only the image of what is happening now. In contrast to the mass media, art institutions are places of historical comparison between the past and present, between the original promise and the contemporary realization of this promise and, thus, they possess the means and ability to be sites of critical discourse—because every such discourse needs a comparison, needs a framework and a technique of comparison. Given our current cultural climate, art institutions are practically the only places where we can actually step back from our own present and compare it with other historical eras. In these terms, the art context is nearly irreplaceable because it is particularly well suited to critically analyze and challenge the claims of the media-driven zeitgeist. Art institutions serve as a place where we are reminded of the entire history of the critique of represen-tation and of the critique of the sublime—so that we can measure our own time against this historical background.

The Hero's Body: Adolf Hitler's Art Theory

Anyone who speaks of heroes and the heroic these days can hardly help but think of Fascism, National Socialism, and Hitler. Fascism elevated the production of the heroic to a political program. But what is a hero? What distinguishes a hero from a nonhero? The heroic act transforms the hero's body from a medium into a message. In that respect the hero's body is distinct from that of the politician, scientist, entrepreneur, or philosopher, the bodies of whom are concealed behind the social function they exercise. When a body manifests itself directly, however, when it explodes the shell of the social roles it usually plays, the result is the hero's body. Such explosive bodies were exalted and exhibited for example by the Italian Futurists. They cast off the artist's traditional role of supplier to the art market, of producer of images, and instead made their own bodies the image. And these were not bodies at rest; they were battling, enthusiastic, emotionalized, vibrating, explosive bodies—that is to say, heroic. The heroes of antiquity had such bodies, when they were seized by an unbridled passion and were ready to destroy or be destroyed. Italian Fascism and German National Socialism adopted the artistic program of making the medium of the body the message, and they made the message a political one. They sided not with convictions, theories, and programs, but with bodies—those of athletes, fighters, and soldiers.

Making the body the message requires above all an arena, a stage—or, alternatively, it requires modern reporting, a public created by the media. That is why today we are experiencing a widespread return of the heroic, even if it is not always explicitly avowed, because we live in a world theater in which everything ultimately depends entirely on the body. In this world theater, all discourses are reduced to sound bites, slogans, and exclamations. Today's media stars become stars entirely by means of their bodies, not by what they say or do. These are the bodies of athletes that make it evident that they are under great exertion, bodies that are involved in a struggle, bodies subject to danger, but also the bodies of rock stars that vibrate with the passion that seizes them, the bodies of models, actors, politicians—and the bodies of suicide bombers who explode along with the bodies of others. Documented, commented on, and celebrated by the media, all these bodies dominate our collective imagination.

Fascism introduced the age of the body, and we continue to live in that age, even though Fascism as a political program has been displaced from the cultural mainstream. Indeed, this very displacement of it as a political program is a sign that we are unable to come to terms with the reality of our own media. Above all we shy away from asking the crucial questions: What distinguishes the heroic body of a media star from the unheroic bodies of the audience? Where lies the magic border that separates the hero from the nonhero on a purely corporeal plane? These questions arise because on the ideological plane a democratic equality of all is postulated that does not in fact exist in the reality of the media. For in today's media-driven democracy, all ideologies, theories, and discourses are equal, indeed—and hence also irrelevant. Yet bodies are all the less equal for that.

National Socialism and Hitler, of course, had an answer for such questions: race. As Hitler said:

> When defending its existence, every race operates from the powers and values that are naturally given to it. Only someone who is suited to be heroic thinks and acts heroically.... Creatures that are by nature purely prosaic—physically unheroic creatures, for example—also demonstrate unheroic features in their struggle for survival. However, just as it is possible, for example, for the unheroic elements of a community to train the heroically inclined to be unheroic, the emphatically heroic can also single-mindedly subordinate other elements to its own tendency.

With this ideology in mind, Hitler observed that the German people, because it is composed of "various racial substances," cannot be characterized unconditionally as heroic, since it must be admitted "that the normal span of our abilities is determined by the inherent racial composition of our Volk." Yet Hitler was not satisfied with that observation, and he defined National Socialism as follows: "It wants the political and cultural leadership of our Volk to take on the face and expression of the race whose heroism that is rooted in its racial nature first created the German Volk out of a conglomerate of its various elements. National Socialism thus commits itself to a heroic teaching regarding the value of blood, race, and personality as well of the eternal laws of selection. . . ."[1]

Consequently, Hitler saw himself as a trainer, a coach for the German people. Like the Jedi Knights from the *Star Wars* epic, he sought hidden, racially determined forces that had to be discovered and mobilized in the body of the German Volk. Films of more recent years are absolutely teeming with such trainer figures. Countless kung fu teachers in all sorts of films—from the cheapest B movies to *Matrix* or *Kill Bill*—try to get their charges to forget everything they have learned, heard, and thought and to trust only the inherent, hidden instincts of their bodies in order to discover the powers to which their bodies are genetically destined. In real life, as well, thousands upon thousands of advisers teach athletes, politicians, and entrepreneurs to trust themselves, to act spontaneously and instinctively, to discover their own bodies. The discovery of one's own body has thus become the greatest art of our age.

In the Third Reich this art was declared to be the official art of the State. For Hitler said: "Art is a sublime mission that obliges one to fanaticism."[2] And also: "Art can never be separated from the human being. . . . Even if other aspects of life can still be learned through some form of education, art must be innate."[3] For Hitler, true art consists in revealing the heroic race, the heroic body, and bringing it to power. This art, of course, is possible only for those who are themselves by nature heroically endowed, for this kind of true art is itself a heroic mission. The artist thus becomes one with the hero. Therefore Hitler saw art not simply as a depiction of the heroic but as an act that is itself heroic because it gives shape to reality, to the life of the Volk. And this act, which is also an act of the body, because it cannot be separated from the body of the person performing it, is the work of an artist-hero that should and must be valid not only for the present but for all time. In Hitler's view, unheroic "modern" art can never acquire this eternal value because it does not manifest a heroic determination on the level of the artist's body, but instead tries to support itself on a theory, on a discourse, on notions of international style and fashion. Consequently, modern art betrays and fails its higher mission, since theory, discourse, and criticism are superficial phenomena characteristic only of the age that tends to neglect and conceal the body of the artist.

This is why Hitler declared that the liberation of art from its imprisonment by an art criticism that argues in terms of pure theory would be the main task of his policies on art—and he was committed to pursuing this battle for liberation as ruthlessly as possible. He wanted to produce instead a heroic art that possessed eternal value. One could admittedly say that this constant emphasis on art's eternal value was mere talk, merely rhetorical flourishes meant to justify the regime's atrocities. That view loses plausibility, however, when one notes that Hitler used the same arguments to move the members of his own party to sacrifice their immediate political goals in order to create art that would have eternal value, asking them: "Can we allow ourselves to sacrifice for art at a time when there is so much poverty, want, misery, and despair everywhere around us?"[4] The answer, of course, is "Yes, we can and should"—and therefore Hitler denounced the lack of appreciation for art by those members of the National Socialist Party who were not willing to mobilize the means and forces of the Third Reich not just for the economy and the army but for art as well. Because, so Hitler argued, the Third Reich could exist eternally only if it were to produce art that possessed eternal value. And there is no doubt that Hitler saw the perspective of eternity alone as a State's ultimate justification. Hence the production of art with eternal value was the ultimate task of politics if politics hoped to pass the crucial test—the test of eternity. The concept of eternity was thus the core of Hitler's reflections on heroic art—on art as a heroic act. The heroic was nothing other than a willingness to live for eternal fame and to exist in eternity. The heroic act was defined by its transcendence of immediate, temporal goals and was an eternal role model for all time to come. Given its centrality and influence, it makes sense for us to look at this concept of eternity in detail.

First of all, Hitler never spoke of eternity in the sense of the immortality of the individual soul. The eternity of which Hitler spoke was a post-Christian one, a thoroughly modern one in that it was a purely material, corporeal eternity—an eternity of ruins, of the relics left behind by any civilization once it has gone under. These material remains that outlast every civilization could produce in later observers either fascination, astonishment, at the recognition of the traces of a heroic, artistic, creative act, or simply tired disinterest. Thus Hitler understood the eternal value of art as the impression that art makes on a future observer. And it was this gaze of the future observer that Hitler sought to please first and foremost—and from it Hitler expected to receive an approving aesthetic judgment of the monuments of that past which was Hitler's own present. Hence Hitler viewed his own present from an archeological perspective—from the perspective of a future archaeologist and *flâneur* with an interest in art—and from that perspective Hitler anticipated ultimate aesthetic recognition. This archaeological perception of his own present linked Hitler with a sensibility widely held in his day. The question of how their own present would eventually be seen in the historical perspective moved many writers and artists of modernity.

At the same time, however, Hitler parted with the mainstream of artistic modernism on this very point. The typical modern artist is a reporter, an observer of the modern world who informs others about his or her observations. In this sense, the modern artist is moving on the same plane on which a theoretician, critic, or writer moves. Hitler, by contrast, did not want to observe; he wanted to be observed. And he wanted not only to be observed but to be admired, even idolized, as a hero. He understood art, artists, and artworks as objects of admiration—not as the subjects of observation or analysis. For him, observers, viewers, critics, writers, and archaeologists were always other people. And thus for Hitler the crucial question became: How could he as artist-hero hold his own against the judgment of the future observer, the future archaeologist? What could he do to ensure that his present work would be admired and idolized in the indeterminate, indefinable future of eternity? The future observer is a great unknown, who initially has no immediate access to the artist's soul, who does not know the artist's intentions and motives—and thus who can scarcely be influenced by theoretical discourse or political propaganda of the past. Future observers will pass judgment exclusively on the basis of the external, corporeal, material appearance of the artwork; its meaning, content, and original interpretational framework will be necessarily alien to them. For Hitler, the recognition of art as art is not, therefore, a matter of a spiritual tradition, of a culture that is transferred from one subject to another, from one generation to another. And for that reason alone, Hitler should be seen as a product of radical modernity, because he no longer believed that culture could be "spiritually" handed down across time. Since the death of God, in Hitler's view, the spirit of culture, the spirit of tradition, and hence any possible cultural meaning or significance had become finite and mortal. The eternity of which Hitler spoke is thus not a spiritual eternity but a material one—an eternity beyond culture, beyond spirit. And hence the question of the eternal value of art becomes one of material constitution, one of the body of its observer.

Thus Hitler by no means understood the search for the heroic in art to be a superficial stylization of the glorious past. He vehemently rejected a purely external, formalistic imitation of the past that tried to apply obsolete artistic styles borrowed from the vocabulary of art history to the products of technical modernity. Hitler recognized that such attempts were themselves a regression into the past that would lead artists astray from the true goal of achieving an artistic perfection adequate to their own historical time. Hitler was full of irony when remarking on such regressive trends. In his polemics against them, he liked to use arguments that the representatives of modernism—in his view, "the Jews"—customarily used in such cases. Thus he said that

> the National Socialist state must defend itself against the sudden appearance of those nostalgic people who believe they have an obligation to offer the National Socialist revolution a "theutsche Kunst" with an h [i.e., "German art," with an archaic spelling—Trans.] as a binding legacy for the future handed down by the muddled world of their own romantic conceptions. They have never been National Socialists. Either they lived in the hermitages of a Germanic dream world that the Jews always found ridiculous, or they trotted piously and naively amid the heavenly crowds of a bourgeois Renaissance.... Thus today they offer train stations in genuine German Renaissance style, street signs and typefaces in Gothic letters, song lyrics freely adapted from Walther von der Vogelweide, fashions based on Gretchen and Faust . . . No, gentlemen! . . . Just as in other aspects of our lives, we gave free rein to the German spirit to develop, in this sphere of art too we cannot do violence to the modern age in favor of the Middle Ages.[5]

The very question of which style was appropriate to the art of the Third Reich is one Hitler considered fundamentally wrong, because he considered style to be a catchword that corrupted art just as much as the concept of the new did. For Hitler, an artwork is good only if it achieves perfection in its response to a specific, very concrete, present-day challenge—and not when it presents itself as an example of a universal style, old or new. But how does a viewer determine that this concrete artwork has achieved a specific, concrete result with the greatest possible perfection? How can art be produced and appreciated at all if all known criteria of aesthetic judgment, both new and old, "medieval" or "modern," are considered invalid and even detrimental to art? To make the correct aesthetic judgment, the viewer simply needs to have certain taste—namely, good, correct, precise taste. That is: in order to judge an artwork adequately without using any additional explanations, theories, and interpretations, the person judging must have "eternal" taste, if you will—taste that outlasts the ages. And the artists themselves have to possess such taste as well if they want their works to continue to be judged valid beyond their own time. At this point it becomes clear how art can become eternal: Art that is valid for the ages can be produced only when, first, the artist has the same taste as the viewer, and, second, when it is guaranteed that this taste will endure the ages. All attempts to escape this fundamental requirement of stabilizing the aesthetic taste that binds both the artist and the viewer are firmly rejected by Hitler. Neither discourse nor education comes into question for him as a possible mediator between artist and viewer, because such things are always superficial, conventional, and temporal. Only an inherent identity, prior to all reflection, between the taste of the artist and the taste of a possible viewer can guarantee that the artwork will be perceived as perfect.

But how can someone—artist or viewer—come into possession of such an inherent taste that both joins and binds if all taste is dependent on its time? That was the central question of Hitler's art theory, and his answer to this question was race. Only the concept of race enabled Hitler to postulate the possibility of a purely inherent, nontheoretical, nondiscursive unity between artist and viewer. And indeed: The course of modern art has constantly been fraught with complaints about its dependence on commentary, of its being overburdened by theory. Even today, there are regular calls to dismiss all theories, all interpretations, and all discourses and finally concentrate on the pure perception of the artwork. In general, however, these unceasing demands to devote ourselves to the pure perception of art leave unanswered the question of what guarantee there could be that this kind of perception of art can take place at all. How can one look at art and react to it if one has never been informed by any means of discourse that there is such a phenomenon as art? And how can such utterly uninformed perception lead to an aesthetic judgment about an artwork's value when there is no discourse that links the artist's creation to the viewer's appreciation of it? It seems that it is indeed only a theory of race that could explain to us how art can be perceived beyond all theory.

For race theory transposes the whole analysis from the level of discourse to the level of the body. In Hitler's view, the artwork is not a statement but a body that is derived from another body, namely, the body of the artist. The appreciation of art is, therefore, an effect of direct contact between two bodies: the body of the artwork and the body of the viewer. Everything that relates to art thus plays out on a purely corporeal level. And so one might say that the viewer can identify the artist's artwork and adequately perceive it independently of all discourses only because the viewer's body is similar in structure to that of the artist—and therefore it is equipped with the same purely corporeal reactions to external stimuli. And the artistic taste consists of the totality of these instinctive corporeal reactions. Hence one could say that human beings are able to identify and enjoy human art only because the producer and consumer belong to the same race—namely, the human race. By contrast, if we credit this theory, extraterrestrials would not be in a position to identify, perceive, and enjoy human art because they lack the necessary affiliation with the human race, the human body, and human instincts. Of course, Hitler did not believe that humanity was composed entirely of a single race, since there were substantial factual differences in the judgments of taste made by different people. Consequently, he presumed that humanity was composed of different races, and thus people have different tastes because they belong to different races. And that means that for art to be eternal, the body itself must possess an eternal component. And this eternal component of the body, the eternity immanent to the body itself, is race. Only the viewer who is racially endowed with a heroic attitude can recognize the heroic element in the art of the past.

Thus, in Hitler's view, race theory and art theory form an inherent, indivisible unity. In the end, races exist because they are necessary to explain how art can be transhistorical—that is, why future generations can enjoy the art of the past. Race theory is a theory of the autonomy of art in relation to history, to culture, and to art criticism. In fact, the faith that in questions of art it ultimately comes down to the body is indeed a thoroughly modern faith. It is our era's widespread response to the death of God—understood as the death of the spirit, of reason, of theory, of philosophy, of science, of history. Reference to this sort of immediate corporeal response to art usually serves today also as a reason to reject any interpretive discourse on art as a falsification of art, that is, as a falsification of the spontaneous reaction of the spectator's body to the artwork. And quite a number of modern and contemporary authors would agree with the opening statement of one of Hitler's speeches that he made in the year 1937: "One of the signs of the decay of culture we have experienced in the recent past is the abnormal growth of art theoretical writing."[6]

For Hitler, establishing the eternal value of art could be reached only by stabilizing the racial inheritance that would guarantee the correct reaction of the future spectator's body to art. Here lies the true originality of Hitler's theory of art: He moved the discussion from the level of the artist's production to the level of the spectator's production. For him, therefore, it was less about producing good art—that already exists, after all—than about producing the mass of viewers who will react correctly to this art even in the distant future. The true artwork that the Third Reich wanted to produce was a viewer of art who was in a position to recognize and appreciate the heroic element in art. For, once again, Hitler by no means understood an artwork to be a passive depiction of the hero. For him, and in this respect he is a child of modernity, the artist is a hero. The act of artistic creation is in itself an active, heroic act, no matter whether it is the creation of an artwork or the creation of a State. The more magnificent this creative act is, the more clearly evident is the heroism of its creator, since such an act is, as we have said, not a spiritual act but a purely corporeal one. The creations of a heroic race can be observed and admired in the monuments produced by the bodies that belong to that race. The ultimate artwork, however, is the viewer whom the heroic politics makes into a member of the heroic race. The true art of politics is, for Hitler, the art of the continuous production of heroic bodies.

The practical consequences of the artistic efforts that Hitler made in this direction are well known, and little need be said about them. Perhaps this will suffice: In terms of art, this work presented itself exclusively as a work of reduction, of destruction, of regression. To put it another way, as soon as he had an opportunity to operate with the body of the Volk and with the State in an artistic way, he immediately began to follow the very program that, on the theoretical plane, he had polemically blamed on modern, "degenerate" art. The true activity of the Third Reich consisted in the constant annihilation of human beings or the continuous reduction of them to the level of "bare life," as Giorgio Agamben called it. All of the constructive intentions, all the programs for centuries of racial breeding that were supposed to produce a heroic race remained pure theory in the end.

Historically, Hitler embodies exemplarily the figure of a loser who was unable to bring to conclusion anything he started—not even the work of reduction and annihilation. Amazingly, Hitler succeeded in losing utterly, not only politically and militarily but also morally—something that is almost unique as a historical achievement, for defeat in real life is usually balanced by moral victory and vice versa. As an absolute loser in this sense, Hitler holds a certain fascination for our time, because modern art has always celebrated the figure of the loser—this is the very penchant for which Hitler condemned modern art so vehemently. We have learned to admire the figure of the *poète maudit* and the *artiste raté* who earned their places as heroes of the modern imagination not by victory but by spectacular defeat. And in the competition among losers that modern culture has offered us, Hitler was exceptionally, if inadvertently, successful.

Educating the Masses: Socialist Realist Art

From the beginning of the 1930s until the fall of the Soviet Union, Socialist Realism was the only officially recognized creative method for all Soviet artists. The plurality of competing aesthetic programs that characterized Soviet art in the 1920s came to an abrupt end when the Central Committee issued a decree on April 23, 1932, disbanding all existing artistic groups and declaring that all Soviet creative workers should be organized according to profession in unitary "creative unions" of artists, architects, and so on. Socialist Realism was proclaimed the obligatory method at the First Congress of Writers Union in 1934 and was subsequently expanded to encompass all the other arts, including the visual arts, without any substantial modification of its initial formulations. According to the standard official definition, Socialist Realist artwork must be "realistic in form and Socialist in content." This apparently simple formulation is actually highly enigmatic. How can a form, as such, be realistic? And what does "Socialist content" actually mean? To translate this vague formulation into a concrete artistic practice was not an easy task, and yet the answers to those questions defined the fate of every individual Soviet artist. It determined the artist's right to work—and in some cases his or her right to live.

During the initial, Stalinist period of the formation of Socialist Realism, the numbers of artists, as well as artistic devices and styles, that were excluded from the Socialist Realist canon continually expanded. Since the middle of the 1930s, officially acceptable methods were defined in an increasingly narrow way. This politics of narrow interpretation and rigorous exclusion lasted until the death of Stalin in 1952. After the so-called thaw and partial de-Stalinization of the Soviet system, which began at the end of the '50s and continued until the dissolution of the Soviet Union, the interpretation of Socialist Realism became more inclusive. But the initial politics of exclusion never allowed a truly homogeneous or even coherent Socialist Realist aesthetic to emerge. And the subsequent politics of inclusion never led to true openness and artistic pluralism. After the death of Stalin, an unofficial art scene emerged in the Soviet Union but it was not accepted by the official art institutions. It was tolerated by the authorities, but works made by these artists were never exhibited or published, showing that Socialist Realism never became inclusive enough.

Soviet Socialist Realism was intended to be a rigorously defined artistic style, but it was also intended to be a unified method for all Soviet artists, even those working in different media, including literature, the visual arts, theater, and cinema. Of course, these two intentions were mutually contradictory. If an artistic style cannot be compared with other artistic styles in the same medium, its aesthetic specificity as well as its artistic value remains unclear. For Soviet artists, the main point of reference was the bourgeois West. The main concern of the Soviet ideological authorities was that Soviet Socialist art not look like the art of the capitalist West, which was understood as a decadent, formalist art that rejected the artistic values of the past. In contrast, the Soviets formulated a program that appropriated the artistic heritage of all past epochs: Instead of rejecting the art of the past, artists should use it in the service of the new Socialist art. The discussion regarding the role of artistic heritage in the context of the new Socialist reality that took place at the end of the 1920s and the beginning of the '30s was decisive in terms of the future development of Socialist Realist art. It marked an essential shift from the art of the '20s, which was still dominated by modernist, formalist programs, toward the art of Socialist Realism, which was concerned primarily with the content of an individual artwork.

The attitude of avant-garde artists and theoreticians toward artistic heritage was powerfully expressed in a short but important text by Kazimir Malevich, "On the Museum," in 1919. At that time, the new Soviet government feared that the old Russian museums and art collections would be destroyed by civil war and the general collapse of state institutions and the economy. The Communist Party responded by trying to secure and save these collections. In his text, Malevich protested against this pro-museum policy by calling on the state not to intervene on behalf of the art collections because their destruction could open the path to true, living art. In particular, he wrote:

> Life knows what it is doing, and if it is striving to destroy one must not interfere, since by hindering we are blocking the path to a new conception of life that is born within us. In burning a corpse we obtain one gram of powder: accordingly

thousands of graveyards could be accommodated on a single chemist's shelf. We can make a concession to conservatives by offering that they burn all past epochs, since they are dead, and set up one pharmacy.

Later, Malevich gives a concrete example of what he means:

The aim (of this pharmacy) will be the same, even if people will examine the powder from Rubens and all his art—a mass of ideas will arise in people, and will be often more alive than actual representation (and take up less room).[1]

Malevich believed that new, revolutionary times should be represented by new, revolutionary art forms. This opinion was, of course, shared by many other artists on the "left front" in the 1920s. But their critics argued that true revolution takes place not on the level of artistic forms but rather on the level of their social use. Being confiscated from the old ruling classes, appropriated by the victorious proletariat, and put at the service of the new Socialist state, old artistic forms become intrinsically new because they were filled with a new content and used in a completely different context. In this sense, these apparently old forms became even more new than the forms that were created by the avant-garde but used in the same context by bourgeois society. This proto-postmodern criticism of "formalist trends in art" was formulated by an influential art critic of that time, Yakov Tugendkhol'd, in the following way: "The distinction between proletarian and non-proletarian art happens to be found not in form but in the idea of use of this form. Locomotives and machines are the same here as in the West; this is our form. The difference between our industrialism and that of the West, however, is in the fact that here it is the proletariat that is the master of these locomotives and machines; this is our content."[2] During the 1930s this argument was repeated again and again. The artists and theoreticians of the Russian avant-garde were accused of taking a nihilistic approach toward the art of the past, preventing the proletariat and the Communist Party from using their artistic heritage for their own political goals. Accordingly, Socialist Realism was presented initially as an emergent rescue operation directed against the destruction of cultural tradition. Years later Andrei Zhdanov, a member of the Politbureau who was at that time responsible for official cultural politics, said in a speech dedicated to questions of art:

Did the Central Committee act "conservatively," was it under the influence of "traditionalism" or "epigonism" and so on, when it defended the classical heritage in painting? This is sheer nonsense!...We Bolsheviks do not reject the cultural heritage. On the contrary, we are critically assimilating the cultural heritage of all nations and all times in order to choose from it all that inspire the working people of Soviet society to great exploits in labor, science, and culture.[3]

The discussion of the role of artistic heritage set the framework for the development of the aesthetics of Socialist Realism, because it indicated some formal criteria that a Socialist Realist artwork should satisfy in order to be both Socialist and Realist. The introduction of Socialist Realism initiated a long and painful struggle against formalism in art in the name of a return to classical models of art-making. In this way, Socialist Realist art was increasingly purged of all traces of modernist "distortions" of the classical form—so that at the end of this process it became easily distinguishable from bourgeois Western art. Soviet artists also tried to thematize everything that looked specifically Socialist and non-Western—official parades and demonstrations, meetings of the Communist Party and its leadership, happy workers building the material basis of the new society. In this sense, the apparent return to a classical mimetic image effectuated by Socialist Realism was rather misleading. Socialist Realism was not supposed to depict life as it was, because life was interpreted by Socialist Realist theory as being constantly in flux and in development—specifically in "revolutionary development," as it was officially formulated.

Socialist Realism was oriented toward what had not yet come into being but what it saw should be created and was destined to become a part of the Communist future. Socialist Realism was understood as a dialectical method. "What is most important to the dialectical method," wrote Stalin, "is not that which is stable at the present but is already beginning to die, but rather that which is emerging and developing, even if at present it does not appear stable, since for the dialectical method only that which is emerging and developing cannot be overcome."[4] Of course, it was the Communist Party that had the right to decide what would die and what could emerge.

The mere depiction of the facts was officially condemned as "naturalism," which should be distinguished from "realism," taken to imply an ability to grasp the whole of historical development, to recognize in the present world the signs of the coming Communist world. The ability to make the correct, Socialist selection of current and historical facts was regarded as the most important quality of a Socialist artist. Boris Ioganson, one of the leading official artists of the Stalin period, said in his speech to the First Convention of Soviet Artists in the 1930s: "A fact is not the whole truth; it is merely the raw material from which the real truth of art must be smelted and extracted—the chicken must not be roasted with its feathers."[5] And he argued further that the locus of creativity in the art of Socialist Realism is not the technique of painting but the "staging of the picture"—which is to say that the painter's work does not essentially differ from the photographer's. A Socialist Realist painting is a kind of virtual photography—meant to be realistic, but to encompass more than a mere reflection of a scene that actually happened. The goal was to give to the image of the future world, where all the facts would be the facts of Socialist life, a kind of photographic quality, which would make this image visually credible. After all, Socialist Realism had to be realist only in form and not in content.

The apparent return to the classical was misleading as well. Socialist Realist art was not created for museums, galleries, private collectors, or connoisseurs. The introduction of Socialist Realism coincided with the abolishment of the free market, including the art market. The Socialist State became the only remaining consumer of art. And the Socialist State was interested only in one kind of art—socially useful art that appealed to the masses, that educated them, inspired them, directed them. Consequently, Socialist Realist art was made ultimately for mass reproduction, distribution, and consumption—and not for concentrated, individual contemplation. This explains why paintings or sculptures that looked too good, or too perfect on the traditional criteria of quality, were also regarded by the Soviet art critic as "formalist." Socialist Realist artwork had to refer aesthetically to some acceptable kind of heritage, but at the same time it had to do so in a way that opened this heritage to a mass audience, without creating too great a distance between an artwork and its public.

Of course, many traditional artists who felt pushed aside by the Russian avant-garde of the 1920s undoubtedly exploited the change in political ideology to achieve recognition for their work. Many Soviet artists still painted landscapes, portraits, and genre scenes in the tradition of the nineteenth century. But the paintings of such leading Socialist Realist artists as

Alexander Deineka, Alexander Gerassimov, or even Isaak Brodsky referred primarily to the aesthetics of posters, color photography, or the cinema. In fact, the successful pictures made by these artists could be seen throughout the country, reproduced on countless posters and in endless numbers of books. They were popular "hits"—and it would be wide of the mark to criticize a pop song for having lyrics that were not great poetry. A capability for mass distribution became the leading aesthetic quality in Stalinist Russia. Even if painting and sculpture dominated the system of visual arts, both were produced and reproduced on a mass scale comparable only to photo-graphic and cinematic production in the West. Thousands and thousands of Soviet artists repeated the same officially approved Socialist Realist subjects, figures, and compositions, allowing themselves only the slightest variations on these officially established models, variations that remain almost unnotice-able by an uninformed viewer. The Soviet Union therefore became saturated with painted and sculpted images that seemed to be produced by the same artist.

Socialist Realism emerged at a time when global commercial mass culture achieved its decisive breakthrough and became the determining force that it has remained ever since. Official culture in the Stalin era was a part of this global mass culture, and it fed on the expectations it awakened world-wide. And an acute interest in new media that could be easily reproduced and distributed was widespread in the 1930s. In their various ways, French Surrealism, Belgian Magic Realism, German Neue Sachlichkeit, Italian Novecento, and all other forms of realism of the time exploited images and techniques derived from the vastly expanding mass media of the day. But in spite of these resemblances, Stalinist culture was structured differently from its counterpart in the West. Whereas the market dominated, even defined, Western mass culture, Stalinist culture was noncommercial, even anti-commercial. Its aim was not to please the greater public but to educate, to inspire, to guide it. (Art should be realist in form and socialist in content, in other words.) In practice, this meant that art had to be accessible to the masses on the level of form, although its content and goals were ideologically deter-mined and aimed at reeducating the masses.

In his 1939 essay "Avant-garde and Kitsch" Clement Greenberg famously attempted to define the difference between avant-garde art and mass culture (which he termed "kitsch"). Mass kitsch, he stated, uses the effects of art, whereas the avant-garde investigates artistic devices.[6] Accordingly, Greenberg placed the Socialist Realism of the Stalin era, as well as other forms of totalitarian art, on a par with the commercial mass culture of the West. Both, he averred, aimed to exert the maximum effect on their audiences, rather than engaging critically with artistic practices themselves. For Greenberg, the avant-garde ethos thus entailed a distant and critical attitude toward mass culture. But in fact, the artists of the classical European and Russian avant-garde were very much attracted to the new possibilities offered by the mass production and dissemination of images. The avant-garde actually disapproved of only one aspect of commercial mass culture: its pandering to mass taste. Yet modernist artists also rejected the elitist "good" taste of the middle classes. Avant-garde artists wished to create a new public, a new type of human being, who would share their own taste and see the world through their eyes. They sought to change humankind, not art. The ultimate artistic act would be not the production of new images for an old public to view with old eyes, but the creation of a new public with new eyes.

Soviet culture under Stalin inherited the avant-garde belief that humanity could be changed and thus was driven by the conviction that human beings are malleable. Soviet culture was a culture for masses that had yet to be created. This culture was not required to prove itself economically—to be profitable, in other words—because the market had been abolished in the Soviet Union. Hence the actual tastes of the masses were completely irrelevant to the art practices of Socialist Realism, more irrelevant, even, than they were to the avant-garde, since members of the avant-garde in the West, for all their critical disapproval, had to operate within the same economic conditions as mass culture. Soviet culture as a whole may therefore be understood as an attempt to abolish that split between the avant-garde and mass culture that Greenberg diagnosed as the main effect of art operating under the conditions of Western-style capitalism.[7] Accordingly, all other oppositions related to this fundamental opposition—between production and reproduction, original and copy, quality and quantity, for instance—lost their relevance in the framework of Soviet culture. The primary interest of Socialist Realism was not an artwork but a viewer. Soviet art was produced in the relatively firm conviction that people would come to like it when they had become better people, less decadent and less corrupted by bourgeois values. The viewer was conceived of as an integral part of a Socialist Realist work of art and, at the same time, as its final product. Socialist Realism was the attempt to create dreamers who would dream Socialist dreams.

To promote the creation of a new humankind, and especially of a new public for their art, artists joined forces with those in political power. This was undoubtedly a dangerous game for artists to play, but the rewards appeared at the beginning to be enormous. The artist tried to attain absolute creative freedom by throwing off all moral, economic, institutional, legal, and aesthetic constraints that had traditionally limited his or her political and artistic will. But after the death of Stalin all utopian aspirations and dreams of absolute artistic power became immediately obsolete. The art of official Socialist Realism became simply a part of the Soviet bureaucracy—with all the privileges and restrictions connected to this status. Soviet artistic life after Stalin became a stage on which the struggle against censorship was played out. This drama had many heroes who managed to widen the framework of what was allowed, to make "good artworks," or "truly realistic artworks," or even "modernist artworks" on the borderline of what was officially possible. These artists and the art critics who supported them became well known and were applauded by the greater public. Of course, this struggle involved a lot of personal risk that in many cases led to very unpleasant consequences for the artists. But still it is safe to say that within the post-Stalinist art of Socialist Realism a new value system had established itself. The art community valued not the artworks that defined the core message and the specific aesthetics of Socialism Realism, but rather the artworks that were able to widen the borders of censorship, to break new ground, to give to other artists more operative space. At the end of this process of expansion Socialist Realism lost its borders almost completely and disintegrated, together with the Soviet state.

In our time the bulk of Socialist Realist image production has been reevaluated and reorganized. The previous criteria under which these artworks were produced have become irrelevant: neither the struggle for a new society nor the struggle against censorship is a criterion any longer. One can only wait and see what use the contemporary museum system and contemporary art market will make of the heritage of Socialist Realism—of this huge number of artworks that were initially created outside of, and even directed against, the modern, Western art institutions.

Beyond Diversity: Cultural Studies and Its Post-Communist Other

One can safely say that the cultural situation in the countries of post-Communist Eastern Europe is still a blind spot for contemporary cultural studies. Cultural studies has, that is, some fundamental difficulties in describing and theorizing the post-Communist condition. And, frankly, I do not believe that a simple adjustment of the theoretical framework and vocabulary of cultural studies to the realities of Eastern Europe—without reconsideration of some of the discipline's fundamental presuppositions—would be sufficient to enable its discourse to describe and discuss the post-Communist reality. I will now try to explain why such an adjustment seems to be so difficult.

The currently dominant theoretical discourse in the field of cultural studies has a tendency to see historical development as a road that brings the subject from the particular to the universal, from premodern closed communities, orders, hierarchies, traditions, and cultural identities toward the open space of universality, free communication, and citizenship in a democratic modern state. Contemporary cultural studies shares this image with the venerable tradition of the European Enlightenment—even if the former looks at this image in a different way and, accordingly, draws different conclusions from the analysis of this image. The central question that arises under these presuppositions is namely the following: How are we to deal with an individual person traveling along this road—here and now? The traditional answer of liberal political theory, which has its origins in French Enlightenment thought, is well known: the person on this road has to move forward as quickly as possible. And if we see that a certain person is not going fast enough—and maybe even takes a rest before moving ahead—then appropriate measures must be taken against this person, because such a person is holding up not only his or her own transition but also the transition of the whole of humankind to the state of universal freedom. And humankind cannot tolerate such slow movement because it wants to be free and democratic as soon as possible.

This is the origin of the liberal mode of coercion and violence in the name of democracy and freedom. And it is very much understandable that today's cultural studies wants to reject this kind of coercion and to defend the right of the individual subject to be slow, to be different, to bring his or her premodern cultural identity into the future as legitimate luggage that may not be confiscated. And, indeed, if the perfect, absolute democracy is not only unrealized, but also unrealizable, then the way that leads to it is an infinite one—and it makes no sense to force the homogeneity and universality of such an infinite future on the heterogeneous cultural identities here and now. Rather, it is better to appreciate diversity and difference, to be more interested in where the subject is coming from than in where he or she is going to. So we can say that the present strong interest in diversity and difference is dictated in the first place by certain moral and political considerations—namely, by the defense of the so-called underdeveloped cultures against their marginalization and suppression by the dominating modern states in the name of progress. The ideal of progress is not completely rejected by contemporary cultural thought. This thought, rather, strives to find a compromise between the requirements of modern uniform democratic order and the rights of premodern cultural identities situated within this general order.

But there is also one aspect in all this which I would like to stress. The discourse of diversity and difference presupposes a certain aesthetic choice—I mean here a purely aesthetic preference for the heterogeneous, for the mix, for the crossover. This aesthetic taste is, in fact, very much characteristic of the postmodern art of the late 1970s and '80s—that is, during the time that the discipline of cultural studies emerged and developed to its present form. This aesthetic taste is ostensibly very open, very inclusive—and in this sense also genuinely democratic. But, as we know, postmodern taste is by no means as tolerant as it seems to be at first glance. The postmodern aesthetic sensibility in fact rejects everything universal, uniform, repetitive, geometrical, minimalist, ascetic, monotonous, boring—everything gray, homogeneous, and reductionist. It dislikes Bauhaus, it dislikes the bureaucratic and the technical; the classical avant-garde is accepted now only on the condition that its universalist claims are rejected and it becomes a part of a general heterogeneous picture.

And, of course, the postmodern sensibility strongly dislikes—and *must* dislike—the gray, monotonous, uninspiring look of Communism. I believe that this is, in fact, why the post-Communist world today remains a blind spot. Western spectators trained in certain aesthetics and conditioned by a certain artistic sensibility just do not want to look at the post-Communist world because they do not like what they see. The only things that contemporary Western spectators like about the post-Communist—or still Communist— East are things like Chinese pagodas, or old Russian churches, or Eastern European cities that look like direct throwbacks to the nineteenth century—all things that are non-Communist or pre-Communist, that look diverse and different in the generally accepted sense of these words and that fit well within the framework of the contemporary Western taste for heterogeneity. On the contrary, Communist aesthetics seems to be not different, not diverse, not regional, not colorful enough—and, therefore, confronts the dominating pluralist, postmodern Western taste with its universalist, uniform Other.

But if we now ask ourselves: What is the origin of this dominating postmodern taste for colorful diversity?—there is only one possible answer: the market. It is the taste *formed by* the contemporary market, and it is the taste *for* the market. In this respect, it must be recalled that the emergence of the taste for the diverse and the different was directly related to the emergence of globalized information, media, and entertainment markets in the 1970s and the expansion of these markets in the '80s and '90s. Every expanding market, as we know, produces diversification and differentiation of the commodities that are offered on this market. Therefore, I believe that the discourse and the politics of cultural diversity and difference cannot be seen and interpreted correctly without being related to the market-driven practice of cultural diversification and differentiation in the last decades of the twentieth century. This practice opened a third option for dealing with one's own cultural identity—beyond suppressing it or finding a representation for it in the context of existing political and cultural institutions. This third option is to sell, to commodify, to commercialize this cultural identity on the international media and touristic markets. It is this complicity between the discourse of cultural diversity and the diversification of cultural markets that makes a certain contemporary postmodern critical discourse so immediately plausible and, at the same time, so deeply ambiguous. Although extremely critical of the homogeneous space of the modern state and its institutions, it tends to be uncritical of contemporary heterogeneous market practices—at least, by not taking them seriously enough into consideration.

Listening to postmodern critical discourse, one has the impression of being confronted with a choice between a certain universal order incorporated by the modern state, on the one hand, and fragmented, disconnected, diverse "social realities" on the other. But, in fact, such diverse realities simply do not exist—and the choice is a completely illusory one. The apparently fragmented cultural realities are, in fact, implicitly connected by the globalized markets. There is no real choice between universality and diversity. Rather, there is a choice between two different types of universality: between the universal validity of a certain political idea and the universal accessibility obtained through the contemporary market. Both—the modern state and the contemporary market—are equally universal. But the universality of a political idea is an openly manifested, articulated, visualized universality that demonstrates itself immediately by the uniformity and repetitiveness of its external image. On the other hand, the universality of the market is a hidden, nonexplicit, nonvisualized universality that is obscured by commodified diversity and difference.

So we can say that postmodern cultural diversity is merely a pseudonym for the universality of capitalist markets. The universal accessibility of heterogeneous cultural products which is guaranteed by the globalization of contemporary information markets has replaced the universal and homogeneous political projects of the European past—from the Enlightenment to Communism. In the past, to be universal was to invent an idea or an artistic project that could unite people of different backgrounds, that could transcend the diversity of their already existing cultural identities, that could be joined by everybody—if he or she would decide to join them. This notion of universality was linked to the concept of inner change, of inner rupture, of rejecting the past and embracing the future, to the notion of *metanoia*—of transition from an old identity to a new one. Today, however, to be universal means to be able to aetheticize one's identity as it is—without any attempt to change it. Accordingly, this already existing identity is treated as a kind of readymade in the universal context of diversity. Under this condition, becoming universal, abstract, uniform makes you aesthetically unattractive and commercially inoperative. As I have already said, for contemporary tastes, the universal looks too gray, boring, unspectacular, unentertaining, uncool to be aesthetically seductive.

And that is why the postmodern taste is fundamentally an antiradical taste. Radical political aesthetics situates itself always at the "degree zero" (*degré zéro*) of literary and visual rhetoric, as Roland Barthes defined it[1]—and that means also at the degree zero of diversity and difference. And this is also why the artistic avant-garde—Bauhaus, and so on—seem to be so outmoded today: These artistic movements embody an aesthetic sensibility for the political, not for the commercial market. There can be no doubt about it: every utopian, radical taste is a taste for the ascetic, uniform, monotonous, gray, and boring. From Plato to the utopias of the Renaissance to the modern, avant-garde utopias—all radical political and aesthetic projects presented themselves always at the degree zero of diversity. And that means: One needs to have a certain aesthetic preference for the uniform—as opposed to the diverse—to be ready to accept and to endorse radical political and artistic projects. This kind of taste must be, obviously, very unpopular, very unappealing to the masses. And that is one of the sources of the paradox that is well known to the historians of modern utopias and radical politics. On the one hand, these politics are truly democratic because they are truly universal, truly open to all—they are by no means elitist or exclusive. But, on the other hand, they appeal, as I said, to an aesthetic taste that is relatively rare. That is why radical democratic politics presents itself often enough as exclusive, as elitist. One must be committed to radical aesthetics to accept radical politics—and this sense of commitment produces relatively closed communities united by an identical project, by an identical vision, by an identical historical goal. The way of radical art and politics does not take us from closed premodern communities to open societies and markets. Rather, it takes us from relatively open societies to closed communities based on common commitments.

We know from the history of literature that all past utopias were situated on remote islands or inaccessible mountains. And we know how isolated, how closed the avant-garde movements were—even if their artistic programs were genuinely open. Thus we have here a paradox of a universalist but closed community or movement—a paradox which is truly modern. And that means, in the case of radical political and artistic programs, we have to travel a different historical road than the one described by standard cultural studies: It is not a road from a premodern community to an open society of universal communication. Rather, it is a road from open and diverse markets toward utopian communities based on a common commitment to a certain radical project. These artificial, utopian communities are not based on the historical past; they are not interested in preserving its traces, in continuing a tradition. On the contrary, these universalist communities are based on historical rupture, on the rejection of diversity and difference in the name of a common cause.

On the political and economic level, the October Revolution effectu-ated precisely such a complete break with the past, such an absolute destruc-tion of every individual's heritage. This break with every kind of heritage was introduced by the Soviet power on the practical level by abolishing private property and transferring every individual's inheritance into the collective property. Finding a trace of one's own heritage in this undifferentiated mass of collective property has become as impossible as tracing the individual incinerated objects in the collective mass of ashes. This complete break with the past constitutes the political as well as the artistic avant-garde. The notion of the avant-garde is often associated with the notion of progress. In fact, the term "avant-garde" suggests such an interpretation because of its military connotations—initially, it referred to the troops advancing at the head of an army. But to Russian revolutionary art, this notion began to be applied habitually since the 1960s.

The Russian artists themselves never used the term avant-garde. Instead, they used names like Futurism, Suprematism, or Constructivism—meaning not moving progressively toward the future but being already situated in the future because the radical break with the past had already taken place, being at the end—or even beyond the end—of history, understood in Marxist terms as a history of class struggle, or as a history of different art forms, different art styles, different art movements. Malevich's famous *Black Square*, in par-ticular, was understood as the degree zero both of art and of life—and because of that, as the point of identity between life and art, between artist and artwork, between spectator and art object, and so on.

The end of history is understood here not in the same way as Francis Fukuyama understands it.[2] The end of history is brought about not by the final victory of the market over every possible universal political project but, on the contrary, by the ultimate victory of a political project, which means an ultimate rejection of the past, a final rupture with the history of diversity.

It is the radical, the apocalyptic end of history—not the kind of end-of-history as is described by contemporary liberal theory. That is why the only real heritage of today's post-Communist subject—its real place of origin—is the complete destruction of every kind of heritage, a radical, absolute break with the historical past and with any kind of distinct cultural identity. Even the name of the country "Russia" was erased and substituted by a neutral name lacking any cultural tradition: Soviet Union. The contemporary Russian, post-Soviet citizen thus comes from nowhere, from the degree zero at the end of every possible history.

Now it becomes clear why it is so difficult for cultural studies to describe the way that post-Communist countries and populations evolved after the demise of Communism. On the one hand, this path of evolution seems to be the familiar, well-worn path from a closed society to an open society, from the community to a civil society. But the Communist community was in many ways much more radically modern in its rejection of the past than the countries of the West. And this community was closed not because of the stability of its traditions but because of the radicality of its projects. And that means: the post-Communist subject travels the same route as described by the dominating discourse of cultural studies—but he or she travels this route in the opposite direction, not from the past to the future, but from the future to the past; from the end of history, from posthistorical, postapocalyptic time, back to historical time. Post-Communist life is life lived backward, a movement against the flow of time. It is, of course, not a completely unique historical experience. We know of many modern apocalyptic, prophetic, religious communities which were subjected to the necessity of going back in historical time. The same can be said of some artistic avant-garde movements, and also of some politically motivated communities that arose in the 1960s. The chief difference is the magnitude of a country like Russia, which must now make its way back—from the future to the past. But it is an important difference. Many apocalyptic sects have committed collective suicide because they were incapable of going back in time. But such a huge country as Russia does not have the option of suicide—it has to proceed backward whatever collective feelings it has about it.

It goes without saying that the opening of the Communist countries has meant for their populations, in the first place, not democratization in political terms but the sudden necessity of surviving under new economic pressures dictated by international markets. And this also means a return to the past, because all Communist countries of Eastern Europe, including Russia, had their capitalist past. But until very recently, the only acquaintance most of the Russian population had with capitalism was mainly via pre-revolutionary, nineteenth-century Russian literature. The sum of what people knew about banks, loans, insurance policies, or privately owned companies was gleaned from reading Tolstoy, Dostoyevsky, and Chekhov at school—leaving impressions not unlike what people often feel when they read about ancient Egypt. Of course, everyone was aware that the West was still a capitalist system; yet they were equally aware that they themselves were not living in the West, but in the Soviet Union. Then suddenly all these banks, loans, and insurance policies began to sprout up from their literary graves and become reality; so for ordinary Russians it feels now as if the ancient Egyptian mummies had risen from their tombs and were now reinstituting all their old laws.

Beyond that—and this is, probably, the worst part of the story—the contemporary Western cultural markets, as well as contemporary cultural studies, require that the Russians, Ukrainians, and so on rediscover, redefine, and manifest their alleged cultural identity. They are required to demonstrate, for example, their specific Russianness or Ukrainness, which, as I have tried to show, these post-Communist subjects do not have and cannot have because even if such cultural identities ever really existed they were completely erased by the universalist Soviet social experiment. The uniqueness of Communism lies in the fact that it is the first modern civilization that has historically perished—with the exception, perhaps, of the short-lived Fascist regimes of the 1930s and '40s. Until that time, all other civilizations that had perished were premodern; therefore they still had fixed identities that could be documented by a few outstanding monuments like the Egyptian pyramids. But the Communist civilization used only those things that are modern and used by everyone—and, in fact, non-Russian in origin. The typical Soviet emblem was Soviet Marxism. But it makes no sense to present Marxism to the West as a sign of Russian cultural identity because Marxism has, obviously, Western and not Russian origins. The specific Soviet meaning and use of Marxism could function and be demonstrated only in the specific context of the Soviet state. Now that this specific context has dissolved, Marxism has returned to the West—and the traces of its Soviet use have simply disappeared. The post-

Communist subject must feel like a Warhol Coca-Cola bottle brought back from the museum into the supermarket. In the museum, this Coca-Cola bottle was an artwork and had an identity—but back in the supermarket the same Coca-Cola bottle looks just like every other Coca-Cola bottle. Unfortunately, this complete break with the historical past and the resultant erasure of cultural identity are as difficult to explain to the outside world as it is to describe the experience of war or prison to someone who has never been at war or in prison. And that is why, instead of trying to explain his or her lack of cultural identity, the post-Communist subject tries to invent one—acting like Zelig in the famous Woody Allen movie.

This post-Communist quest for a cultural identity that seems to be so violent, authentic, and internally driven is, actually, a hysterical reaction to the requirements of international cultural markets. Eastern Europeans want now to be as nationalistic, as traditional, as culturally identifiable as all the others—but they still do not know how to do this. Therefore, their apparent nationalism is primarily a reflection of and an accommodation to the quest for otherness that is characteristic of the cultural taste of the contemporary West. Ironically, this accommodation to the present international market requirements and dominating cultural taste is mostly interpreted by Western public opinion as a "rebirth" of nationalism, a "return of the repressed," as additional proof corroborating the current belief in otherness and diversity. A good example of this mirror effect—the East reflecting Western expectations of "otherness" and confirming them by artificially simulating its cultural identity—is the reshaping of Moscow's architecture that took place almost immediately after the demise of the Soviet Union.

In the relatively brief period since the Soviet Union was disbanded, Moscow—once the Soviet, now the Russian capital—has already undergone an astonishingly rapid and thorough architectural transformation. A lot has been built in this short time, and the newly constructed buildings and monuments have redefined the face of the city. The question surely is, in what manner? The answer most frequently advanced in texts by Western observers and in some quarters of today's more earnest Russian architectural criticism is that Moscow's architecture is kitschy, restorative, and above all eager to appeal to regressive Russian nationalist sentiments. In the same breath, these commentators claim to make out a certain discrepancy between Russia's embrace of capitalism and the regressive, restorative aesthetics now evident in the Russian capital. The reason most often provided for this alleged contradiction is that, in view of the current wave of modernization and the host of economic and social pressures brought in its wake, these restorative aesthetics are intended as a compensatory measure through their evocation of Russia's past glory.

Without question, the aesthetic profile of contemporary Moscow is unambiguously restorative; although one encounters a few borrowings from contemporary Western architecture, these references are always situated in a historicist, eclectic context. In particular, the most representative buildings of Moscow's new architecture are those that signal a programmatic rejection of the contemporary international idiom. Yet in Russia, as was already mentioned, capitalism is already experienced as restorative, that is, as the return from the country's socialist future back to its pre-revolutionary, capitalist past. This in turn means that, rather than contradicting it, restorative architecture is actually complicit with the spirit of Russian capitalism. According to Russian chronology, modernism is a feature of the Socialist future, which now belongs to the past, rather than being part of the capitalist past, which is now the future. In Russia, modernism is associated with Socialism—and not, as it is in the West, with progressive capitalism. This is not merely because modernist artists often voiced Socialist views, but also a result of modernism's concurrence with a period when Socialism prevailed in Russia— which means, in fact, with the entire twentieth century. That is why the new Moscow architecture wants to signal the return of the country to pre-revolutionary times, for example, to the nineteenth century, by abandoning the modernism of the twentieth century.

Furthermore, Russians associate modernism above all with Soviet architecture of the 1960s and '70s, which by and large they utterly detested. During these decades, vast urban zones sprung up all over the Soviet Union, stocked with enormous, highly geometrical, standardized residential buildings of a gray and monotonous appearance and entirely bereft of artistic flair. This was architecture at the bottom line. Modernism in this guise is now spurned since it is felt to combine monotony and standardization and embody Socialism's characteristic disregard for personal taste. As it happens, similar arguments can be heard today in a like-minded rejection of the oppositional and modernistically inclined dissident culture of the 1960s and '70s, whose proponents nowadays find approval for the most part only in the West. In Russia, the former dissident culture is dismissed for still being "too Soviet"—in other words, for being too arrogant, intolerant, doctrinaire, and modernist. Instead, the current *cause célèbre* in Russia is postmodernism. Thus, the postmodernist return of nineteenth-century eclecticism and historicism is currently celebrated in Russia as signaling the advent of true pluralism, openness, democracy, and the right to personal taste—as the immediate visual confirmation that the Russian people feel liberated at last from the moralistic sermons of Communist ideology and the aesthetic terror of modernism.

But, contrary to this rhetoric of diversity, inclusiveness, and liberation of personal taste, the new Moscow style is, in fact, wholly the product of centralized planning. Today's most representative and stylistically influential buildings have come about on the initiative of the post-Soviet mayor of Moscow, Yuri Luzhkov, and his preferred sculptor, Zurab Tsereteli. As was also the case with Stalinist architecture, which likewise was the result of close cooperation between Stalin and a small coterie of carefully appointed architects, this is an example of a most typically Russian phenomenon—a case, namely, of planned and centralized pluralism. The current Moscow style has distanced itself from the modernist monotony of the 1960s and '70s to the same degree as Stalinist architecture was divesting itself of the rigorism of the Russian avant-garde. The Moscow style is a revival of a revival. But most importantly, this return to popular taste and aesthetic pluralism in both cases ultimately proved to be a state-sponsored *mise-en-scène*.

The way this kind of controlled pluralism functions is well illustrated by a concrete example, the reconstruction of the Cathedral of Christ the Savior in the center of Moscow, a project which was just recently completed. This rebuilt cathedral is already counted as the most important post-Soviet architectural monument in Moscow today. More than anyone else, Luzhkov has prioritized the reconstruction of the cathedral as the city's most prestigious project. A few historical details should shed light on the implications of this restoration project.

The original Cathedral of Christ the Savior was built by the architect Konstantin Ton between 1838 and 1860 as a symbol of Russia's victory over the Napoleonic army; it was demolished on Stalin's orders in 1931. Immediately after its completion, the disproportionately huge cathedral was roundly criticized and ridiculed as monumental kitsch. This original view was shared by all subsequent architectural opinion, which was probably a further reason for the later decision to blow it up—it simply was deemed to be of little artistic value. At the same time, this demolition amounted to an intensely symbolic political act, since in spite of—or rather precisely due to—its kitschy character, the cathedral was immensely popular with the people, as well as being the most vivid expression of the power held by the Russian Orthodox Church in pre-revolutionary Russia. Hence its demolition came as the climax of the anticlerical campaign being waged in the late 1920s and '30s, which is why it has left such an indelible trace on popular memory.

Given its symbolic status, Stalin designed the square that had been cleared by the cathedral's demolition to be a site for the construction of the Palace of the Soviets, which was envisaged as the paramount monument to Soviet Communism. The Palace of the Soviets was never built—just as the Communist future that it was meant to commemorate was never realized. Yet the design of the palace, drafted by Boris Iofan in the mid-1930s and, only after numerous revisions, approved by Stalin, is still regarded—justly— as the most notable architectural project of the Stalin era. For although the Palace of the Soviets was never actually erected, the project itself served as a prototype for all Stalinist architecture thereafter. This is particularly conspicuous in the notorious Stalinist skyscrapers built in the postwar years that even now largely dominate Moscow's skyline. Just as official ideology at that time claimed that Communism was being prepared and prefigured by Stalinist culture, Stalin's skyscrapers were assembled around the nonexistent Palace of the Soviets in order to herald its advent. However, in the course of de-Stalinization during the 1960s, this locale was given over to build a gigantic open-air swimming pool, the Moskva, in lieu of the palace; and, like the Cathedral of Christ the Savior, it subsequently enjoyed enormous popularity. The pool was kept open even in the winter; and for several months each year vast clouds of steam could be seen from all around, lending the entire prospect the air of a subterranean hell. But this pool can also be viewed as a place where Moscow's population could cleanse themselves of the sins of their Stalinist past. One way or another, it is precisely its memorable location that makes this swimming pool the most dramatic embodiment of the "modernist" cultural consciousness of the 1960s and '70s: It represents a radical renunciation of any type of architectural style, it is like swimming free beneath a clear sky, the "degree zero" of architecture.

Following the dissolution of the Soviet Union, the swimming pool was emptied and replaced by an exact replica of the demolished Cathedral of Christ the Savior. Just how true to the original this copy in fact is has become a highly debated and contentious issue in Russia. But ultimately, all that counts is the underlying intention, which unquestionably is to construct the nearest possible replica of the demolished church—which functions symbolically as an exact copy of the historical past, of Russian cultural identity. Far from being a monument to the new Russian nationalism or a symptom of the resurrection of anti-Western sentiment, the rebuilding of the cathedral was designed to celebrate the defeat of the Soviet universalist, modernist, avant-garde past and the return to the folkloristic Russian identity, an identity that can be easily inscribed in the new capitalist international order. And at first glance, such a symbolic return to national identity seems to be especially smooth in this case: during the entire Soviet period, the site of the cathedral remained, as I said, a void, a blank space—like a white sheet of paper that could be filled with every kind of writing. Accordingly, to reconstruct the old cathedral on its former site, there was no need to remove, to destroy any existing buildings. The Soviet time manifests itself here as an ecstatic interruption of historical time, as a pure absence, as materialized nothingness, as a void, a blank space. So it seems that if this void disappears, nothing will be changed: the deletion will be deleted, and a copy will become identical with the original—without any additional historical losses.

But in fact, this reconstruction demonstrates that the movement to the past—as, earlier, the movement to the future—only brings the country again and again to the same spot. And this spot, this point from which the panorama of Russian history can be seen in its entirety has a name: Stalinism. The culture at the time of Stalin was already an attempt to reappropriate the past after a complete revolutionary break with it—to find in the historical garbage pit left behind by the Revolution certain things that could be useful for the construction of the new world after the end of history. The key principle of Stalinist dialectical materialism, which was developed and sealed in the mid-1930s, is embodied in the so-called *law of the unity and the struggle of opposites*. According to this principle, two contradictory statements can be simultaneously valid. Far from being mutually exclusive, "A" and "not A" must be engaged in a dynamic relationship: in its inner structure, a logical contradiction reflects the real conflict between antagonistic historical forces, which is what constitutes the vitally dynamic core of life. Thus, only statements that harbor inner contradictions are deemed "vital" and hence true. That is why Stalin-era thinking automatically championed contradiction to the detriment of the consistent statement.

Such great emphasis on contradictoriness was of course a legacy dialectical materialism had inherited from Hegel's dialectic. Yet in the Leninist-Stalinist model, as opposed to Hegel's postulates, this contradiction could never be historically transcended and retrospectively examined. All contradictions were constantly at play, remained constantly at variance with one another, and constantly made up a unified whole. Rigid insistence on a single chosen assertion was counted as a crime, as a perfidious assault on this unity of opposites. The doctrine of the unity and the struggle of opposites constitutes the underlying motif and the inner mystery of Stalinist totalitarianism—for this variant of totalitarianism lays claim to unifying absolutely all conceivable contradictions. Stalinism rejects nothing: it takes everything into its embrace and assigns to everything the position it deserves. The only issue that the Stalinist mindset finds utterly intolerable is an intransigent adherence to the logical consistency of one's own argument to the exclusion of any contrary position. In such an attitude, Stalinist ideology sees a refusal of responsibility toward life and the collective, an attitude that could only be dictated by malicious intentions. The basic strategy of this ideology can be said to operate in the following manner: If Stalinism has already managed to unite all contradictions under the sheltering roof of its own thinking, what could be the point of partisanly advocating just one of these various contrary positions? There can ultimately be no rational explanation for such behavior, since the position in question is already well looked after within the totality of Stalinist ideology. The sole reason for such a stubborn act of defiance must consequently lie in an irrational hatred of the Soviet Union and a personal resentment of Stalin. Since it is impossible to reason with someone so full of hatred, regrettably the only remedy available is reeducation or elimination.

This brief detour into the doctrine of Stalinist dialectical materialism allows us to formulate the criterion that intrinsically determined all artistic creativity during the Stalin era: Namely, each work of art endeavored to incorporate a maximum of inner aesthetic contradictions. This same criterion also informed the strategies of art criticism in that period, which always reacted allergically whenever a work of art was found to be expressing a clearly defined, consistently articulated, and unambiguously identifiable aesthetic position—the actual nature of this position was considered secondary. Contrary to the explicit and aggressive aesthetics of the artistic avant-garde, the aesthetic of the Stalin era never defined itself in positive terms. Neither Stalinist ideology nor Stalinist art politics is in any sense "dogmatic." Rather, Stalinist state power acts as an invisible hand behind the heterogeneity, diversity, and plurality of individual artistic projects—censoring, editing, and combining these projects according to its own vision of the ideologically appropriate mix. This means that the symbolic void on which the new-old cathedral was built is not such a blank space after all. It is an invisible, internal space of power hidden behind the diversity of artistic forms. That is why, in the present context, it became so easy to coordinate—if not to identify—this invisible hand of Stalinist state power with the invisible hand of the market. Both operate in the same space behind the diverse, heterogeneous, pluralistic surface. Far from signifying a rebirth of Russian cultural identity, the cathedral's copy in the center of Moscow symbolizes a revival of Stalinist cultural practices under the new market conditions.

This example of the revival of Soviet Stalinist aesthetics as an effect of postmodern taste, which I have tried to elaborate at some length, illustrates a certain point on the relationship between art and politics. Art is, of course, political. All attempts to define art as autonomous and to situate it above or beyond the political field are utterly naive. But having said that, we should not forget that art cannot be reduced to a specific field among many other fields that function as arenas for political decisions. It is not enough to say that art is dependent on politics; it is more important to thematicize the dependence of political discourses, strategies, and decisions on aesthetic attitudes, tastes, preferences, and predispositions. As I have tried to show, radical politics cannot be dissociated from a certain aesthetic taste—the taste for the universal, for the degree zero of diversity. On the other hand, liberal, market-oriented politics is correlated with the preference for diversity, difference, openness, and heterogeneity. Today, the postmodern taste still prevails. Radical political projects have almost no chance today of being accepted by the public because they do not correlate with the dominant aesthetic sensibility. But the times are changing. And it is very possible that in the near future a new sensibility for radical art and politics will emerge again.

Privatizations, or Artificial Paradises of Post-Communism

The term that without a doubt best characterizes the processes that have been taking place since the abdication of the Communist regime in Russia, and in Eastern Europe generally, is *privatization*. The complete abolition of private ownership of the means of production was seen by the theoreticians and practitioners of Russian Bolshevism as the crucial prerequisite to building first a Socialist and later a Communist society. Total nationalization of all private property was the only thing that could achieve the total social plasticity that the Communist Party needed to obtain a completely new, unprecedented power to form society. Above all, however, this meant that art was given primacy over nature—over human nature and over nature generally. Only when the "natural rights" of humanity, including the right to private property, were abolished, and the "natural" connections to origin, heritage, and one's "own" cultural tradition severed, could people invent themselves in a completely free and new way. Only someone who no longer has property is free and available for every social experiment. The abolition of private property thus represents the transition from the natural to the artificial, from the realm of necessity to the realm of (political and artistic) freedom, from the traditional state to the *Gesamtkunstwerk*. The great utopians of history, such as Plato, More, and Campanella, had viewed the abolition of private property and associated private interests as a necessary prerequisite for the unconstrained pursuit of a collective political project.

The reintroduction of private property thus represents an equally crucial prerequisite for putting an end to the Communist experiment. The disappearance of a Communist-run state is thus not merely a political event. We know from history that governments, political systems, and power relations have often changed without having substantial effects on private ownership rights. In such cases, social and economic life continued to be structured according to civil law even as political life was being radically transformed. With the fall of the Soviet Union, by contrast, there was no longer a valid social contract. Enormous territories became abandoned wildernesses as far as rights were concerned—as in the Wild West era in the United States— and had to be restructured. That is to say, they had to be parceled, distributed, and opened up to privatization, following rules that neither existed nor could exist. The process of de-Communization of the formerly Communist Eastern European countries may thus be seen as a drama of privatization that naturally played out beyond all the usual conventions of civilization. It is well known that this drama kindled many passions and produced many victims. Human nature, which had previously been suppressed, manifested itself as raw violence in the struggle over the private acquisition of collective assets.

This struggle should not, however, be understood as simply a transition that leads (back) from a society without private property to a society with private property. Ultimately, privatization proves to be just as much an artificial political construct as nationalization had been. The same state that had once nationalized in order to build up Communism is now privatiz- ing in order to build up capitalism. In both cases private property is subor- dinated to the *raison d'état* to the same degree—and in this way it manifests itself as an artifact, as a product of state planning. Privatization as a (re)introduction of private property does not, therefore, lead back to nature— to natural law. The post-Communist state is, like its Communist predecessor, a kind of artistic installation. Hence the post-Communist situation is one that reveals the artificiality of capitalism by presenting the emergence of capitalism as a purely political project of social restructuring (in Russian: *perestroika*) and not as the result of a "natural" process of economic devel- opment. The establishment of capitalism in Eastern Europe, including Russia, was indeed neither a consequence of economic necessity nor one of gradual and "organic" historical transition. Rather, a political decision was made to switch from building up Communism to building up capitalism, and to that end (in complete harmony with classical Marxism) to produce artificially a class of private property owners who would become the principal protagonists of this process. Thus there was no return to the market as a "state of nature" but rather a revelation of the highly artificial character of the market itself.

For that reason, too, privatization is not a transition but a permanent state, since it is precisely through the process of privatization that the private discovers its fatal dependence on the state: private spaces are necessarily formed from the remnants of the state monster. It is a violent dismemberment and private appropriation of the dead body of the Socialist state, both of which recall sacred feasts of the past in which members of a tribe would consume a totem animal together. On the one hand, such a feast represents a privatization of the totem animal, since everyone received a small, private piece of it; on the other, however, the justification for the feast was precisely a creation of the supraindividual identity of the tribe.

This common identity that makes it possible to experience privatization as a collective project is manifested particularly clearly in the art that is being produced in post-Communist countries today. First of all, every artist in any area once under Communism still finds him- or herself under the shadow of the state art that has just gone under. It is not easy for an artist today to compete with Stalin, Ceausescu, or Tito—just as it is probably difficult for Egyptian artists, now as much as ever, to compete with the pyramids. Moreover, collective property under the conditions of "real Socialism" went along with a large reservoir of collective experiences. This is because the numerous political measures undertaken by the Socialist state to shape the population into a new Communist humanity affected this population as a whole. The result was a collective mental territory whose sovereign was the state. Under the rule of the Communist Party every private psyche was subordinated to and nationalized by the official ideology. Just as the Socialist state at its demise made an immense economic area available to private appropriation, so did the simultaneous abolition of official Soviet ideology leave as its legacy the enormous empire of collective emotions that was made available for private appropriation for the purposes of producing an individualist, capitalist soul. For artists today this represents a great opportunity, for when they enter this territory of collective experiences, they are immediately understood by their public. But it also conceals a great risk, since the artistic privatization proves to be as incomplete and as dependent on commonality now as much as ever.

Be that as it may, however, today's post-Communist art is produced largely by means of the privatization of the mental and symbolic territory that has been left behind by the Soviet ideology. Admittedly, it is not unlike the Western art of postmodernism in this respect; for appropriation or, if you will, privatization, continues to function as the leading artistic method in the context of international contemporary art. Most artists today appropriate various historical styles, religious or ideological symbols, mass-produced commodities, widespread advertising, but also the works of certain famous artists. The art of appropriation sees itself as art after the end of history: It is no longer about the individual production of the new but about the struggles of distribution, about the debate over property rights, about the individual's opportunity to accumulate private symbolic capital. All of the images, objects, symbols, and styles appropriated by Western art today originally circulated as commodities on a market that has always been dominated by private interests. Hence in this context appropriative art seems aggressive and subversive—a kind of symbolic piracy that moves along the border between the permitted and the prohibited and explores the redistribution of capital—at least of symbolic capital, if not real capital.

Post-Communist art, by contrast, appropriates from the enormous store of images, symbols, and texts that no longer belong to anyone, and that no longer circulate but merely lie quietly on the garbage heap of history as a shared legacy from the days of Communism. Post-Communist art has passed through its own end of history: not the free-market and capitalist end of history but the Socialist and Stalinist end of history. The true impudence of real Socialism in its Stalinist form, after all, was its assertion that the Soviet Union marked the historical end of the class struggle, of the revolution, and even of all forms of social criticism—that the salvation from the hell of exploitation and war had already occurred. The real circumstances in the Soviet Union were proclaimed to be identical with the ideal circumstances after the final victory of good over evil. The real location in which the Socialist camp had established itself was decreed the site of utopia realized. It requires—and even then it required—no great effort or insight to demonstrate that this was a counterfactual assertion, that the official idyll was manipulated by the state, that the struggle continued, whether it was a struggle for one's own survival, a struggle against repression and manipulation, or the struggle of permanent revolution.

And nevertheless, it would be just as impossible to banish the famous assertion "It is fulfilled" from the world simply by pointing to world's actual injustices and inadequacies. One speaks of the end of history, that is, of the identity between anti-utopia and utopia, of hell and paradise, of damnation and salvation, when one chooses the present over the future because one believes that the future will no longer bring anything new beyond what one has already seen in the past. Above all, one believes it when one witnesses an image or an event that one assumes is of such incomparable radicalness that it can at most be repeated but never surpassed. This may be an image of Christ on the cross, of Buddha beneath the tree, or, in Hegel's case, Napoleon on a horse. However, it could also be the experience of the Stalinist state—of the state that created the most radical form of expropriation, of terror, of total equality, because it was directed against everyone equally. This was precisely the argument of Alexandre Kojève's famous Parisian lectures in the 1930s on Hegel's philosophy of history, as he explicitly declared Stalinism to be the end of history. In the postwar period Kojève's successors began to speak again of the end of history, or *post-histoire* and postmodernism. This time, however, it was no longer Stalinism but the victory of free-market capitalism in the Second World War and later in the cold war that would usher in the final stage of history. And once again the attempt was made to refute the discourse about the end of history by pointing to the continuing progress of history in actuality. But the choice of the present over the future cannot be refuted by factual arguments, since that choice takes both the factual and all arguments that refer to the factual to be merely the eternal recurrence of the same—and hence of that which has been already overcome historically. There is nothing easier than to say that the struggle goes on, since this is obviously the truth of healthy human reason. It is more difficult to recognize that those involved in the struggle are in fact not struggling at all but have simply ossified in battle position.

Thus post-Communist art is an art that passed from one state after the end of history into the other state after the end of history: from real Socialism into postmodern capitalism; or, from the idyll of universal expropriation following the end of the class struggle into the ultimate resignation with respect to the depressing infinity in which the same struggles for distribution, appropriation, and privatization are permanently repeated. Western postmodern art, which reflects on this infinity and at the same time savors it, sometimes wants to appear combative, sometimes cynical, but in any case it wants to be critical. Post-Communist art, by contrast, proves to be deeply anchored in the Communist idyll—it privatizes and expands this idyll rather than renouncing it. That is why post-Communist art frequently seems too harmless, that is, not critical or radical enough. And indeed it pursues the utopian logic of inclusion, not the realist logic of exclusion, struggle, and criticism. It amounts to an extension of the logic of Communist ideology, which sought to be universalist and strove toward dialectical unity of all oppositions but ultimately remained stuck in the confrontations of the cold war because it resisted all symbols of Western capitalism. The independent, unofficial art of late Socialism wanted to think through the end of history more rigorously and to expand the utopia of the peaceful coexistence of all nations, cultures, and ideologies both to the capitalist West and to the pre-Communist history of the past.

Russians artists from the 1960s and 1970s, such as Vitali Komar and Alexander Melamid, and later the Slovenian artists' group Irwin or the Czech artist Milan Kunc, pursued this strategy of rigorous inclusion. They created spaces of an artistic idyll in which symbols, images, and texts perceived as irreconcilable in the political reality of the cold war could live in peaceful coexistence. Also as early as the 1960s and 1970s other artists, such as Ilya Kabakov or Erik Bulatov, mixed gloomy images of daily life in the Soviet Union with the cheerful images of official propaganda. The artistic strategies of ideological reconciliation beyond the trenches of the cold war announced at that time an extended and radicalized utopia that was intended to include their enemies as well. This politics of inclusion was pursued by many Russian and Eastern European artists even after the break up of the Communist regime. One might say that it is the extension of the paradise of real Socialism in which everything is accepted that had previously been excluded, and hence it is a utopian radicalization of the Communist demand for the total inclusion of one and all, including those who are generally considered dictators, tyrants, and terrorists but also capitalists, militarists, and the profiteers of globalization. This kind of radicalized utopian inclusivity was often misunderstood as irony, but it is rather a posthistorical idyll that sought analogies instead of differences.

Even post-Communist poverty is depicted as utopian by today's Russian artists, because poverty unites whereas wealth divides. Boris Mikhailov in particular depicts everyday life in Russia and the Ukraine in a way that is both unsparing and loving. The same idyllic note is perceived clearly in the videos of Olga Chernyshova, Dmitri Gutov, and Lyudmila Gorlova; for these artists, utopia lives on in the daily routine of post-Communism, even if officially it has been replaced by capitalist competition. The gesture of collective political protest, by contrast, is presented as an artistic theatricalization that no longer has a place in the indifferent, utterly privatized daily life of post-Communism. For example, in a performance by the group Radek, a crowd of people crossing the street at an intersection in Moscow's lively downtown is interpreted as a political demonstration by placing the artists, like the revolutionary leaders of the past, in front of this passive crowd with their posters. Once the street has been crossed, however, everyone goes his own way. And Anatoly Ozmolovsky designed his political action in Moscow as a direct citation from the events of 1968 in Paris. The political imagination presents itself here as the storeroom of historical (pre)images that are available for appropriation.

This characterization does not, of course, apply to all the art made in the countries of the former Soviet Union. The reaction to the universalist, internationalist, Communist utopia does not always, or even primarily, consist in the attempt to think through this utopia more radically than was done under the conditions of real Socialism. Rather, people frequently reacted to this utopia with a demand for national isolationism, for the creation of a fixed national and cultural identity. This reaction could also be clearly noted already in the late Socialist phase, but it was intensified sharply after the new national states were created on the territory of the former Soviet Union, former Yugoslavia, and the former Eastern Bloc—and the search for national cultural identities became the main activity of those states. Admittedly, these national cultural identities were themselves cobbled together from appropriated remnants of the Communist empire, but as a rule this fact is not openly acknowledged. Rather, the Communist period is interpreted as a traumatic interruption of an organic historical growth of the national identity in question.

Communism is thus externalized, deinternationalized, and portrayed as the sum of the traumas to which a foreign power subjected one's own identity, which now requires therapy so that said identity can become intact again. For the non-Russian peoples of the former Soviet Union and Eastern Europe, the time of the dominance of the Communist parties is consequently presented as a time of Russian military occupation, under which the peoples in question merely suffered passively. For the theoreticians of Russian nationalism, in turn, Communism was initially the work of foreigners (Jews, Germans,

Latvians, etc.), but it had already been largely overcome during Stalinism and replaced by a glorious Russian empire. Thus the nationalists of all these countries are in complete agreement in their historical diagnosis, and they are prepared for further struggle, even though they repeatedly find themselves on different sides of this struggle. The only thing that falls out of this fortuitous consensus is post-Communist art, or better, postdissident art, which clings to peaceful universalism as an idyllic utopia beyond any struggle.

Europe and Its Others

In recent years we have been hearing European politicians say over and over that Europe is not just a community of economically defined interests but something more—namely, a champion of certain cultural values that should be asserted and defended. But we know of course that in the language of politics "something more" as a rule means "something less." And, indeed, what European politicians really want to say is that Europe cannot and should not expand unlimitedly, but should end where its cultural values end. The concept of culture defines de facto the self-imposed borders of economic and political expansion, for the scope of the applicability of European culture is thus more narrowly defined as the area of European economic interests. Europe will thereby differentiate itself in relation to Russia, China, India, and Islamic countries, but also with respect to its ally the United States, and at the same time present itself as an internally homogeneous community of values that possesses a specific cultural identity to which those who come to Europe should conform, thank you very much. The question I would like to raise here is not whether such a differentiation, such a definition, of European cultural values is desirable or not. Rather, I would like to ask how exactly are European cultural values defined by European politicians today, and how successfully? Second, what interests me is what effect this demand for European cultural identity has on the arts in Europe.

The desire to situate one's own culture in an international comparison is surely completely legitimate. The question is simply how well this attempt succeeds in Europe's case. Now, as a rule, European values are defined as humanistic values that have their origin in the Judeo-Christian legacy and in the tradition of the European Enlightenment. European values are generally thought to include respect for human rights, democracy, tolerance of the foreign, and openness to other cultures. To put it another way, the values that are proclaimed to be specifically European values are in fact universalistic, and one could rightly demand that non-Europeans respect them as well. Therein lies the entire difficulty that inevitably confronts those who would like to define European cultural identity by means of such values or analogous ones: Namely, these values are too general, too universal, to define a specific cultural identity and to differentiate it from other cultures. On the other hand, the catalog of these values is too meager to do justice to the immense wealth of the European cultural tradition. The discourse on European cultural identity has been circulating this paradox for decades now. On the one hand, this circulation evokes the feeling of an enormous intellectual dynamic, but on the other the corresponding discourse remains in the same spot the whole time. The project of defining the particular cultural identity of Europe by appealing to universalistic, humanistic values cannot succeed, if only because it is incoherent on the level of simple logic.

Every logically coherent definition of a cultural identity presumes that other cultures are different but of equal value. If, however, the particular European values are defined as universal humanistic values, that can only mean that other non-European cultures must be considered antihumanistic by nature, that is, as inherently inhuman, antidemocratic, intolerant, and so on. In view of this diagnosis, it is clear that the European cultural and political sensibility is necessarily ambiguous. To the extent that human rights and democracy can be recognized as universal values, Europeans, as champions of such values, feel morally obliged to push them through worldwide. In the process they find themselves, quite rightly, confronted with the accusation that they are pursuing an old European policy of imperialist expansion under the guise of defending and championing human rights. To the extent, however, that human rights can be recognized as particularly European values, Europeans feel obliged to protect themselves within Europe, that is, to isolate the European cultural sphere and defend it against the antihumanistic aliens. Hence European politics oscillates between imperialism and isolationism— mirroring the particular–universal character of the values that it wants to assert as its own.

Quite clearly such a particular–universal definition of European culture places other cultures under immense pressure to justify themselves. Either they are supposed to prove that they have already Europeanized to the point where they have assimilated the universal, humanistic values, or they are supposed to prove that they have their own humanistic traditions whose origin does not necessarily lie in the Judeo-Christian tradition but rather in the Buddhist, Confucian, or Islamic tradition. Both strategies for justification, however, are condemned to a situation where the humanistic values are territorialized in the European cultural sphere from the outset. This territorialization is also a burden for Europeans, because as a result they feel they are compelled to characterize non-European cultures as antihumanist, which seems to contradict their humanistic approach right from the start. They can, in fact, only do this if they no longer believe in the universal dimension of these values and are prepared to accept them as specifically European. As a result Europeans who define themselves as champions of humanistic values feel embarrassed for two reasons: on the one hand, they feel obliged to push these values through worldwide, if necessary by force, which in fact contradicts the humanistic ideal, but on the other hand they tend to doubt the universality of this humanistic ideal to the extent that they conceive these values as merely particular to Europe.

Consequently typical Europeans oscillate between fantasies of omnipotence and a chronic inferiority complex. As soon as they assert humanism as a universal truth, they seem to have the world at their feet, because they embody all of humanity. As soon as they conceive humanism as a specifically European value, however, they see themselves as weak, unfit for combat, easily hurt, unprotected, surrounded by a sea of human rights violations, injustices, horrors—abandoned, defenseless, in the face of the antihumanistic alien. Their own humanism transforms from the highest value to a structural weakness, the crucial disadvantage in the wars between cultures. Because the dominant discourse on European identity asserts both things—that humanistic values are universal and that they are particular to Europe—the European psyche is incurably torn between moral superiority and paranoid fear of the other. I cannot say to what extent this inner turmoil benefits European politics, but without a doubt it is the best possible precondition for European art.

The fate of European humanism is deeply connected to that of European art in at least two respects. First, in keeping with the dominant conventions of the European understanding of art, only that made by human hands can be considered art. Second, works of art are ultimately distinguished from other things only in that they are exclusively contemplated and interpreted, but not practically used. The taboo against using the work of art, against consuming it, is the basis of all European art institutions, including as museums and the art market. The fundamental maxim of humanism that the human being can only be viewed as the end and never the means already suggests that European humanism sees the human being as first and foremost a work of art. Human rights are in fact the rights of art, but applied to human beings. Indeed, in the wake of the Enlightenment, the human being is defined not primarily as a mind or soul but as one body among other bodies, ultimately as one thing among other things. On the level of things, however, there is no concept other than the concept of art that would permit one to give precedence to certain things above all other things, that is, to lend these things a specific dignity of physical inviolability not granted to other things.

That is why the question of what art is, is not, in the context of European culture, a question purely specific to art. The criteria we use to distinguish works of art from other things are, that is, not dissimilar from the criteria we apply to distinguish the human from the inhuman. Both processes—the recognition of certain things as works of art and the recognition of certain bodies, and their postures, actions, and attitudes, as human—are inseparably connected to each other in the European tradition. Thus it comes as no surprise that the concept of biopolitics, which Michel Foucault introduced into the discussion of recent decades and which has been further developed by other authors, especially Giorgio Agamben, had a critical undertone from the beginning. To understand human beings as a kind of animal—more precisely, as livestock—is, almost automatically, to belittle their dignity. That is also true—indeed, especially true—when this understanding makes it easier to take better care of the bodily well-being of this human animal. Human beings can only be truly dignified if they can be conceived as works of art—or better, as works of art that they themselves produce as artists. This concept of the human being is the basis of all humanistic utopias, all of which understand individual human beings, and ultimately the community, the state, as works of art. So the question arises: what are we ready to accept as art, and what criteria do we have for accepting certain things as such? For it would seem that only answering that art is the site of becoming human will permit us to see what human beings really are—that is, those human beings who are granted human rights and can be considered the subjects of democracy.

We know, however, that if we formulate the question in this way, we will not get a clear response to it. Especially over the course of modern art, all of the criteria that could clearly distinguish the work of art from other things have been called into question. One can say that European art has rigorously pursued the path of its own deculturalization. All of the traditional mechanisms for identifying art that are deeply anchored in European culture have been critically questioned and declared inadequate. One after another, waves of the European avant-garde declared to be works of art things that would not have been identified as such previously. This was not, as many think, a question of expanding the concept of art. It was not the case that in the course of the development of art an increasingly more comprehensive, more universal concept of art was formulated, under which the earlier, partial concepts of art might have been subsumed. Neither was it about refuting or overcoming old, supposedly outdated criteria for identifying art, nor about replacing them with other, new criteria; rather, it was about the diversification, differentiation, and multiplication of these criteria.

Sometimes a thing was declared a work of art because it was beautiful, sometimes because it was particularly ugly; sometimes aesthetics played no role whatever; certain things are in museums because they were original for or, conversely, typical of their time; because they record important historical personalities and events, or because their authors refused to depict important historical personalities and events; because they correspond to popular taste, or because they reject popular taste; because they were conceived from the outset as works of art, or because they only became such by being placed in a museum; because they were particularly expensive, or because they were particularly cheap, and so on. And in many cases certain works of art are found in museum collections only because they ended up there by chance, and today's curators have neither the right nor the energy to eliminate them. All of that, and much more, is art for us today. The reasons that we have available to recognize something as art thus cannot be reduced to a concept. That is also why European art cannot be clearly differentiated from that of other cultures. When European museums first began to evolve at the end of the eighteenth and the beginning of the nineteenth centuries, they accepted works of art of both European and non-European origin—once again on the basis of the analogies, oppositions, similarities, and differences that connected all these objects. Our understanding of art is thus determined by the many rhetorical tropes, by the numerous metaphors and metonymies that are constantly crossing the boundary between our own and the other, without eliminating this boundary or deconstructing it. All of the reasons for recognizing something as a work of art are partial, but their overall rhetoric is unmistakably European.

This rhetoric, as we well know, was repeatedly applied to the area of the human as well. From Flaubert, Baudelaire, and Dostoyevsky, by way of Kierkegaard and Nietzsche, to Bataille, Foucault, and Deleuze, European thought has acknowledged as a manifestation of the human much of what was previously considered evil, cruel, and inhuman. Just as in the case of art, these authors and many others have accepted as human not only that which reveals itself as human but also that which reveals itself as inhuman—and precisely because it reveals itself as inhuman. The point for them was not to incorporate, integrate, or assimilate the alien into their own world but, conversely, to enter into the alien and become alien to their own tradition. That these authors, like countless others in the European tradition, cannot easily be integrated into the discourse on human rights and democracy, need not, in my opinion, be demonstrated here. Nevertheless, these authors, perhaps like no others, belong for just that reason to the European tradition, because they manifest an inner solidarity with the other, with the alien, even with the threatening and cruel, that lies much deeper and takes us much farther than a simple concept of tolerance. The work of all these authors is an attempt to diagnose within European culture itself the forces, impulses, and forms of desire that are otherwise territorialized in foreign lands. Hence these authors have shown that the truly unique feature of European cultures consists in permanently making oneself alien, in negating, abandoning, and denying oneself—and doing so in a way more radical than that of any culture we know has ever been able to do. Indeed, the history of Europe is nothing other than the history of cultural ruptures, a repeated rejection of one's own traditions.

This certainly does not mean that the discourse on human rights and democracy is inherently deficient or that it should not be entered into. It merely means that this discourse should not serve the goal of differentiating European culture from other cultures, as, unfortunately, happens more and more frequently today. The others, the aliens are correspondingly identified primarily as those who necessarily lack respect for human rights and the capability for democracy and tolerance if only because these values are considered specifically European by definition. Thus these aliens, as soon as they arrive in Europe, are sent down the infinite path to so-called integration, which can never lead to its goal because the public avowal of European values by aliens is inevitably suspicious, can always be interpreted as lip service that conceals the true, inner conviction rather than revealing it. Aliens today are asked not only to accept outwardly the catalog of supposedly European values but also to "internalize" them—a process whose success can never be judged "objectively" and hence must remain unfinished for all eternity.

If the discourse on human rights and democracy can bring no justice to aliens, then this discourse is also unjust in relation to the true European tradition, because it, as we have shown, ignores everything that does not fit into this discourse. This "accursed" part of the European cultural tradition is thus ordinarily dismissed as "mere art." The tendency in politics to treat art as one of the pretty irrelevancies and to ignore its political relevance is well known. This tendency has even significantly increased today, which is especially implausible, because we now live in a time in which most information is communicated by visual means, including political information. Precisely in connection with the debates over political Islam, which have become acute recently, the role of the visual has increased. Politically explosive problems are ignited almost exclusively by images: Danish cartoons, women behind veils, videos of bin Laden. Islamic fundamentalists address the outside world primarily through the medium of video—despite Islam's supposed hostility to images. But even a much simpler example demonstrates what it is about today: When the question of multiculturalism is discussed on the TV, the visual is inevitably of a street in a European city dominated by passers-by whose skin color differs from that of the "original" European population. This gives the impression that culture here functions de facto as a pseudonym for race. As a result, simply transferring a certain discourse into the visual makes it racist—even if that is not explicitly intended. Thus the dependence of today's politics on the images with which it operates is obvious.

It is part of the traditional repertoire of European art to depict oneself as a dangerous, cruel alien. Thus Nietzsche presented himself as an envoy of the Übermensch and Bataille as a champion of cruel Aztec rituals. This tradition of presenting oneself as an evil outsider began at the very latest with Marquis de Sade and developed during black Romanticism and its cult of the satanic into one of the major traditions of European art. And it was not always restricted to art. Already in the nineteenth century there were many artists and intellectuals who not only had sympathies with terrorism but actively participated in terrorist activities. The fact that a few children and grandchildren of immigrant families from Islamic countries who have grown up in Europe profess a radical, fundamentalist variant of Islam is often interpreted as a sign that these young people were not adequately integrated into European culture. But the question arises whether it is not in fact a sign of the reverse, that they have integrated themselves outstandingly well into European culture—but precisely into the tradition within that culture that calls for "living dangerously." If the tradition of European culture and art is understood in its full diversity and internal contradictoriness, the question of who is integrated into this culture or not takes a completely different shape. Those who are ready to see the cultural heritage of Europe in its entirety will notice that it is enormously difficult and almost impossible to escape this legacy and do something genuinely non-European, genuinely alien to European culture. The power of European culture is precisely that it is constantly producing its other. If there is anything at all that is unique in European culture, it is this ability to produce and reproduce not only oneself but also all the possible alternatives to oneself.

Of course, in recent times we have heard the lament that European art has since lost the ability to violate cultural taboos, to transcend the boundaries of European cultural identity, to influence political life and public awareness. The underestimation in our time of the effect of art on the public consciousness is related above all to the fact that art is identified first and foremost as the art market and the work of art as a commodity. The fact that art functions in the context of the art market and that every work of art is a commodity is beyond doubt. The work of art is, however, not just a commodity but also a statement in public space. Art is also made and exhibited for those who do not wish to purchase it—indeed, they constitute the overwhelming majority of the audience for art. Typical visitors to a public exhibition do not view the art on display as commodities, or only rarely so. Rather, they react to the tools by means of which individual artists position themselves in public space as objects of observation, for today everyone is obliged, one way or the other, to present him- or herself in public space. In the process the number of exhibitions, biennials, triennials, and so on is growing constantly. These numerous exhibitions, in which so much money and energy are invested, are not created in the first place for those who purchase art but rather for the masses, for anonymous visitors who will probably never purchase a painting.

Even the art fairs, which are primarily there for buyers, are transforming more and more into events in urban space that attract people who do not wish to be buyers. In our time the art system is well on its way to becoming part of the very mass culture that for so long it wanted to observe and analyze from a distance. And it is becoming part of mass culture not as the production of individual objects that are traded on the art market but as an exhibition praxis that combines architecture, design, and fashion—just as the guiding intellectual figures of the avant-garde, such as the artists from Bauhaus, Vkhutemas, and others had predicted as early as the 1920s and 1930s. But does that mean that art today has become completely identical with mass culture and has completely lost its ability to transcend its boundaries and thus to reflect on itself?

I do not believe so. Mass culture—or let's call it entertainment—has a dimension that is often overlooked but is extremely relevant to the problems of otherness or alienness. Mass culture addresses everyone simultaneously. A pop concert or film screening creates communities of viewers. These communities are transitory; their members do not know one another; their composition is arbitrary; it remains unclear where all these people came from and where they are going; they have little or nothing to say to one another; they lack a shared identity, a common prehistory that could have produced common memories they could share—and despite all that they are communities. These communities recall the communities of those traveling on a train or airplane. To put it another way, they are radically contemporary communities—much more contemporary than religious communities, political communities, or labor collectives. All those traditional communities emerged historically and presume that their members are linked to one another from the outset by something that derives from their shared past—a shared language, a shared faith, a shared political belief, a shared education that enables them to do a certain job. Such communities always have specific boundaries—and they close themselves off from all those with whom they have no shared past.

Mass culture, by contrast, creates communities irrespective of any shared past—communities with no preconditions, communities of a new type. This is the source of their enormous potential for modernization, which is so often overlooked. But mass culture itself is usually not capable of reflecting on and developing this potential fully, because the communities it creates do not sufficiently perceive themselves as communities. The gaze of audience members at a pop concert or a film screening is directed too much forward—at the stage or the screen—for them to be able adequately to perceive and reflect on the space in which they find themselves and the community of which they have become part. That, however, is precisely the sort of reflection with which advanced art is concerned today, whether installation art or experimental curatorial practice. In all these cases objects are not exhibited in a certain space; rather, space itself becomes the major object of perception, the true artwork.

Within this space the body of individual viewers takes up a certain position, of which these viewers are necessarily aware, because by reflecting on the whole space of the exhibition, they feel compelled to reflect as well on their own position, their own perspective. The duration of a visit to an exhibition is necessarily limited—and that means that the individual perspective of the viewers always remains partial because they lack the time to try out all the possible positions and perspectives that an exhibition space offers them. Viewers of an artistic installation that demands of them an all-embracing gaze at the entire space of this installation do not therefore feel up to the challenge. Today's art of exhibitions and installations is not, however, directed at individual viewers who observe individual works of art one after another but rather at communities of viewers who can take in the whole room simultaneously with their gaze. Art today is thus social and political on a purely formal level, because it reflects on the space of the assembly, on the formation of community, and does so independently of whether an individual artist has a specific political message in mind or not. But at the same time, this contemporary art practice demonstrates the position of the alien in today's culture in a much more adequate way than the standard political discourse does. Because I as an individual cannot take in the whole, I must necessarily overlook something that can only be evident to the gaze of others. These others, however, are by no means separated from me culturally: I can imagine them in my position, just as I can imagine myself in theirs. Here the interchangeability of bodies in space becomes evident—that interchangeability that determines our civilization today as a whole. The familiar and the alien are constantly exchanging places—and this global ballet cannot be stopped at will, because this constant exchange of places offers the only way to distinguish the familiar from the alien that remains open to us.

Notes

The Logic of Equal Aesthetic Rights

1. Alexandre Kojève, *Introduction to the Reading of Hegel*, assembled by Raymond Queneau (Ithaca: Cornell University Press, 1980), pp. 5ff.

2. Ibid., pp. 258ff.

On the New

1. Kazimir Malevich, "On the Museum," in Kazimir Malevich, *Essays on Art*, vol. 1 (New York: George Wittenborn, 1971), pp. 68–72.

2. K. Malevich, "A Letter from Malevich to Benois," in *Essays on Art*, vol. 1, p. 48.

3. Søren Kierkegaard, *Philosophische Brocken* (Düsseldorf/Cologne: Eugen Diederichs Verlag, 1960), pp. 34ff. Translated as *Philosophical Fragments*, ed. and trans. with intro. and notes by Howard V. Hong and Edna H. Hong (Princeton: Princeton University Press, 1998).

4. Douglas Crimp, *On the Museum's Ruins* (Cambridge, Mass.: MIT Press, 1993), p. 58.

5. Arthur Danto, *After the End of Art: Contemporary Art and the Pale of History* (Princeton: Princeton University Press, 1997), pp. 13ff.

6. Thierry de Duve, *Kant after Duchamp* (Cambridge, Mass.: MIT Press, 1998), pp. 132ff.

7. Georg Wilhelm Friedrich Hegel, *Vorlesungen über die Ästhetik*, vol. 1 (Frankfurt: Suhrkamp Verlag, 1970), p. 25: "In allen diesen Beziehungen ist und bleibt die Kunst nach der Seite ihrer höchsten Bestimmung für uns ein Vergangenes."

8. See Boris Groys, "Simulated Readymades by Fischli/Weiss," in *Parkett*, no. 40/41 (1994): 25–39.

On the Curatorship

1. Giorgio Agamben, *Propfanierungen* (Frankfurt: Suhrkamp, 2005), p. 53.

2. Jacques Derrida, *La dissémination* (Paris: Editions du Seuil, 1972), pp. 108f.

3. Orhan Pamuk, *My Name Is Red* (New York: Alfred Knopf, 2001), pp. 109–110.

Art in the Age of Biolitics: From Artwork to Art Documentation

1. See Boris Groys, *Unter Verdacht: Eine Phänomenologie der Medien* (Munich: Carl Hanser Verlag, 2000), pp. 54ff.

2. Giorgio Agamben, *Homo Sacer: Sovereign Power and Bare Life*, trans. Daniel Heller-Roazen (Stanford, Calif.: Stanford University Press, 1998), pp. 166ff.; originally published as *Homo sacer: Il potere sovrano e la nuda vita* (Turin: Giulio Einaudi Editore, 1995).

3. See also Jean-François Lyotard, *The Differend: Phrases in Dispute*, trans. Georges van den Abbeele (Manchester: Manchester University Press; Minneapolis: Minnesota University Press, 1988); originally published as *Le Différend* (Paris: Editions de Minuit, 1983).

4. See *Kollektivnye Deystviya: Pojezdki za gorod, 1977–1998* (Moscow: Ad Marginem, 1998). See also Hubert Klocker, "Gesture and the Object. Liberation as Aktion: A European Component of Performative Art," in *Out of Actions: Between Performance and the Object, 1949–1979* (exh. cat.) (Los Angeles: The Museum of Contemporary Art; Vienna: Österreichisches Museum für Angewandte Kunst; Barcelona: Museu d'Art Contemporani de Barcelona; and Tokyo: Museum of Contemporary Art, 1998–99), pp. 166–167.

5. Walter Benjamin, "The Work of Art in the Age of Mechanical Reproduction," in *Illuminations*, trans. Harry Zohn (London: Fontana, 1992), pp. 214–215. [Translator's note: this English edition is a translation of the second version of Benjamin's essay.]

6. Ibid., p. 214.

7. Walter Benjamin, "Das Kunstwerk im Zeitalter seiner technischen Reproduzierbarkeit," in *Gesammelte Schriften*, vol. 1, pt. 2 (Frankfurt am Main: Suhrkamp Verlag, 1974), p. 437. [Translator's note: this is my translation, from the first version of Benjamin's essay, originally published in an altered French translation in *Zeitschrift für Sozialforschung*, vol. 5, Paris, 1936.]

8. Walter Benjamin, "The Work of Art in the Age of Mechanical Reproduction," in *Illuminations*, p. 217.

9. Walter Benjamin, *Reflections: Essays, Aphorisms, Autobiographical Writings*, ed. Peter Demetz, trans. Edmund Jephcott (New York: Schocken Books, 1986), p. 190; first published as "Der Sürrealismus. Die letzte Momentaufnahme der europäischen Intelligenz," *Die Literarische Welt*, 5(1929): 5–7.

Iconoclasm as an Artistic Device: Iconoclastic Strategies in Film

1. Cf. Boris Groys, "Das leidende Bild/The Suffering Picture," in *Das Bild nach dem Letzten Bild*, ed. Peter Weibel and Christian Meyer (Vienna/Cologne: W. Konig, 1991), pp. 99–111.

2. Kazimir Malevich, "Suprematizm. Mir kak bespredmetnost', ili vechnyy pokoy" (Suprematism: The Non-Objective World, or Eternal Quiet), in Kazimir Malevich, *Sobranie sochineniy*, vol. 3 (Moscow: Gileya, 2000), pp. 69ff.

3. Walter Benjamin, "The Work of Art in the Age of Mechanical Reproduction," in *Illuminations*, trans. Harry Zohn (London: Fontana, 1992).

4. See Gilles Deleuze, *Cinema 2: The Time-Image* (Minneapolis: Athlone, 1989).

5. Mikhail Bakhtin, *Rabelais and His World* (Cambridge, Mass.: MIT Press, 1968).

6. Guy Debord, *The Society of the Spectacle* (New York: Zone Books, 1995).

7. Maurice Merleau-Ponty, *Visible et Non-Visible* (Paris: Gallimard, 1973).

8. Sergei Mikhailovich Eisenstein, *Memuary*, vol. 1 (Moscow: Trud, 1997), pp. 47ff.

9. Boris Groys, *Unter Verdacht. Eine Phänomenologie der Medien* (Munich: Hanser, 2000).

10. See Gilles Deleuze, *Cinema 1: The Movement-Image* (Minneapolis: Athlone, 1986).

The City in the Age of Touristic Reproduction

1. René Descartes, *Discourse on Method and Meditations* (Mineola: Dover, 2003), pp. 9ff.

2. Immanuel Kant, *Critique of Judgment* (Indianapolis, Ind.: Hackett, 1987), p. 99.

3. Ibid., p. 100.

4. Karl Rosenkranz, *Ästetik des Hässlichen* (The aesthetics of the ugly) (Leipzig: Reclam Verlag, 1990), p. 20.

The Hero's Body: Adolf Hitler's Art Theory

1. Adolf Hitler, "Die deutsche Kunst als stolzeste Verteidigung des deutschen Volkes," presentation to the Kulturtagung des Parteitags der NSDAP (Conference on the Cultural

Politics of the National-Socialist German Workers Party) in Nürnberg, September 3, 1933. In Adolf Hitler, *Reden zur Kunst- und Kulturpolitik 1933–1939* (Frankfurt: Revolver-Verlag, 2004), pp. 44–45.

2. Ibid., p. 52.

3. Ibid., p. 47.

4. Adolf Hitler, "Kein Volk lebt länger als Dokumente seiner Kultur," presentation to the Kulturtagung des Parteitags der NSDAP (Conference on the Cultural Politics of the National-Socialist German Workers Party) in Nürnberg, September 11, 1935. In Hitler, *Reden zur Kunst*, p. 83.

5. Adolf Hitler, "Kunst verpflichtet zur Wehrhaftigkeit," presentation to the Kulturtagung des Parteitags (Conference on the Cultural Politics of the National-Socialist German Workers Party) in Nürnberg, September 8, 1934. In Hitler, *Reden zur Kunst*, p. 75.

6. Adolf Hitler, "Die grosse Kulturrede des Führers," presentation to the Kulturtagung des Parteitags der NSDAP (Conference on the Cultural Politics of the National-Socialist German Workers Party) in Nürnberg, September 7, 1937. In Hitler, *Reden zur Kunst*, p. 145.

Educating the Masses: Socialist Realist Art

1. Kazimir Malevich, "On the Museum" (1919), *Essays on Art*, vol. 1 (New York: George Wittenberg, 1971), pp. 68–72.

2. Yakov Tugendkhol'd, *Iskusstvo oktiabr'skoi epokhi* (Leningrad, 1930), p. 4.

3. Andrei A. Zhdanov, *Essays on Literature, Philosophy, and Music* (New York, 1950), pp. 88–89, 96.

4. Quoted in N. Dmitrieva, "Das Problem des Typischen in der bildenden Kunst und Literatur," *Kunst und Literatur*, no. 1 (1953): p. 100.

5. Boris Ioganson, "O merakh uluchsheniia uchebno-metodicheskoi raboty v uchebnykh zavedeniiakh Akademii Khudozhestv SSSR," *Sessii Akademii Khudozhestv SSSR. Pervaia i vtoraia sessiia* (1949): 101–103.

6. Clement Greenberg, *Collected Essays and Criticism*, vol. 1 (Chicago: University of Chicago Press, 1986), pp. 17ff.

7. On the relationship between the Russian avant-garde and Socialist Realism, see Boris Groys, *The Total Art of Stalinism: Avant-Garde, Aesthetic Dictatorship, and Beyond* (Princeton: Princeton University Press, 1992).

Beyond Diversity: Cultural Studies and Its Post-Communist Other

1. Roland Barthes, *Le Degré zero de l'écriture* (Paris: Gouthier, 1965). English trans. By Annette Lavers and Colin Smith, *Writing Degree Zero* (London: Cape, 1967).

2. Francis Fukuyama, *The End of History and the Last Man* (New York: Free Press, 1992).

Sources

"The Logic of Equal Aesthetic Rights," originally published as "La politica de la igualdad de derechos esteticos/The Politics of Aesthetic Equal Rights," in *Resistencia/Resistance*, pp. 48–58, 201–210. Edicion de la Memoria, SITAC, Mexico, 2004. Translated by Steven Lindberg.

"On the New," originally published in *Research Journal of Anthropology and Aesthetics*, no. 38 (autumn 2000): 5–17.

"On the Curatorship," originally published as "The Curator as Iconoclast," in *Cautionary Tales: Critical Curating*, ed. Steven Rand and Heather Kouris (New York: Apexart, 2007), pp. 46–55. Translated by Elena Sorokina.

"Art in the Age of Biopolitics: From Artwork to Art Documentation," originally published as "Kunst im Zeitalter der Biopolitik. Vom Kunstwerk zur Kunstdokumentation," in *Katalog*, ed. Okwui Enwesor et al., pp. 107–113. Documenta 11_Plattform 5. Hatje Cantz, 2002. Translated by Steven Lindberg.

"Iconoclasm as an Artistic Device: Iconoclastic Strategies in Film," originally published in *Iconoclash*, ed. Bruno Latour and Peter Weibel. Cambridge, Mass.: MIT Press, 2002. Translated by Matthew Partridge.

"From Image to Image File—and Back: Art in the Age of Digitalization," originally titled "Art in the Digital Age," lecture given at the Biennial in Sydney, 2006 (unpublished).

"Multiple Authorship," originally published in *The Manifesta Decade: Debates on Contemporary Art Exhibitions and Biennials in Post-Wall Europe*. A Roomade Book. Cambridge, Mass.: MIT Press, 2005. Translated by Steven Lindberg.

"The City in the Age of Touristic Reproduction," originally published in *Cidades*, ed. Alfons Hug, pp. 44–55. 25a Bienal de Sao Paulo. Sao Paulo, 2002.

"Critical Reflections," originally published in *Artforum* (October 1997).

"Art at War," originally published as "The Fate of Art in the Age of Terror," in *Making Things Public: Atmospheres of Democracy*, ed. Bruno Latour and Peter Weibel, pp. 970–977. Cambridge, Mass.: MIT Press, 2005.

"The Hero's Body: Adolf Hitler's Art Theory," originally published as "The Hero's Body," in *(my private) Heroes*, catalog of the exhibition at MARTa (Museum of Art and Design), Herford, 2005.

Sources

"Educating the Masses: Socialist Realist Art," originally published in *Russia!*, pp. 318–323. New York: Guggenheim Museum, 2005.

"Beyond Diversity: Cultural Studies and Its Post-Communist Other," originally published in *Democracy Unrealised*, ed. Okwui Enwesor et al., pp. 303–319. Documenta 11_Plattform 1. Hatje Cantz, 2002.

"Privatizatons, or Artificial Paradises of Post-Communism," originally published in *Privatizations*, an exhibition catalog for the KW Institute for Contemporary Art, Berlin. Frankfurt, 2004. Translated by Steven Lindberg.

"Europe and Its Others." Unpublished. Translated by Steven Lindberg.

www.ingramcontent.com/pod-product-compliance
Lightning Source LLC
Chambersburg PA
CBHW020906180526
45163CB00007B/2645